The Career Salesperson

Recharge Your Drive and Ambition, No Matter What Your Age

Stephan Schiffman

Avon, Massachusetts

DEDICATION

To Chubby Checker

Copyright © 2009, by Stephan Schiffman

Published by
Adams Business, an imprint of Adams Media, an F+W Media Company
57 Littlefield Street
Avon, MA 02322
www.adamsmedia.com

ISBN 10: 1-59869-819-2
ISBN 13: 978-1-59869-819-0

Printed in the United States of America.

J I H G F E D C B A

Library of Congress Cataloging-in-Publication Data
available from the publisher.

This publication is designed to provide accurate and authoritative information with regard to the subject matter covered. It is sold with the understanding that the publisher is not engaged in rendering legal, accounting, or other professional advice. If legal advice or other expert assistance is required, the services of a competent professional person should be sought.
—From a *Declaration of Principles* jointly adopted by a Committee of the American Bar Association and a Committee of Publishers and Associations

Many of the designations used by manufacturers and sellers to distinguish their product are claimed as trademarks. Where those designations appear in this book and Adams Media was aware of a trademark claim, the designations have been printed with initial capital letters.

This book is available at quantity discounts for bulk purchases.
For information, please call 1-800-289-0963.

CONTENTS

ACKNOWLEDGMENTS

Writing a book is a lot like life. The best are shepherded along with the help of friends and mentors. And so it is with this book. I would be remiss if I didn't mention them and my gratitude for their help.

It goes without saying that I am more than joyous to include thoughts from Elie Wiesel, who is not only a Nobel Peace Prize winner, but a noble, honest and righteous human being. Many others offered thoughts on getting old, from the advertising business (Peter Georgescu), the entertainment industry (Gary David Goldberg and Larry Gelbart), the literary world (Robert B. Parker), and scientific research (Bert Vogelstein). That they (and many others who could not be included for lack of space) all took time from their busy schedules is something for which I am extremely grateful.

I am grateful also to my collaborator, Curt Schleier, who has worked with me on my most recent manuscripts. He is, of course, an excellent writer and editor, with several books and hundreds of articles to his credit. He is also an excellent trainer; Curt teaches business writing skills to corporate executives and government executives. He knows how to ask the right questions that force me to hone in on the problems and situations we're discussing at the moment. But most important of all, he is extremely simpatico and a pleasure to work with. I'm proud to call him my friend.

It goes almost without saying that I want to thank my editors at Adams, Peter Archer and Laura Daly.

I'd also like to acknowledge my students. Hundreds of them have stayed in touch, sharing their experiences and ideas with me. Please don't stop now. If you have any ideas, questions, or complaints, visit my website, *www.steveschiffman.com*, and drop me a line. I answer all my e-mail and look forward to our dialogue.

Last—but certainly far from least—this is for Anne, Jennifer, and Danielle, whose support and love keep me going.

INTRODUCTION

We are at the start of the largest generational shift in the history of this country—perhaps even the history of the world. America is getting older, and as a nation we are unprepared for it.

Social security, health care, and the need for additional facilities targeted to the needs of the elderly are all issues we seem to be putting off. The attitude of our public officials seems to be: We'll take care of that next year.

This makes it more imperative than ever that Americans as individuals prepare for the future.

And for the record, I don't consider this just an "American" problem. I recently met a man from Manchester, England, who pretty much had his entire pension wiped out by a bankruptcy and the decline in the stock market. So, instead of retiring as planned, he had to go back to work—and his wife, a headmistress at a school—had to continue working longer than she'd planned.

Let me make clear, however: this book isn't how to prepare for retirement. There are plenty of those around already. This book is intended to show you how to prepare—starting as early as age forty—to maximize the later years of your professional life. As you get older, everything starts to change: your body, your outlook toward work and life, even the way people look at you.

This book will show you how to avoid the malaise of aging, how to rekindle your enthusiasm, to stay young at work, and if need be hunt for another job.

No group will be more affected by this generational upheaval than salespeople. On the surface that seems illogical. Why salespeople more so than, say, scientists or teachers?

Part of the reason is the particular nature of sales. It is a highly competitive field that usually doesn't have an off season. If a salesperson isn't working, earning commissions, he or she won't be paid. This constant stress, the need to always produce, is wearing. And the older you get, the less able you are to deal with the pressure.

Another reason is the nature of the people drawn to the field. The best salespeople have a fire in the belly. Selling isn't just a job. For them, it's almost a way of life. They believe in what they do. They believe in their product line. They believe they are performing a useful service. They are always on. So it is much easier for salespeople to burn out earlier than other professions.

TIRED OF 6 A.M. FLIGHTS TO DULUTH

Related to that is what I call the Ted Williams Effect. People say Williams's managerial career was short lived because everything came so naturally to him. He couldn't explain the process of hitting to a youngster because he just stepped up to the plate and did it. It was difficult for him to understand why others couldn't do that as easily as he did.

It's the same thing with good salespeople. They manage themselves pretty well but often have difficulty managing others, in part because of that intensity. How do you explain prospecting or presentations, things that seem so easy and obvious because they come naturally to you? This manifests itself in several ways. Often, salespeople promoted to management find they don't enjoy it and return to sales. Or they turn down promotions because they prefer working in the field, not behind a desk.

As a result, the folks often promoted to senior sales positions are people with business degrees but little practical knowledge of sales. They are very often younger than the best people they supervise, people with years of experience on the firing line and all the wisdom that accrues from that experience.

So it can be emotionally and mentally debilitating to find yourself at age forty or older reporting to a kid who couldn't hold your socks in the field. Not only are the bosses getting younger, but the customers are too. A salesperson may find it difficult to decide whether to give the prospect a spiel or a bottle of formula.

And, let's face it, not only is everyone else around you getting younger, but you're getting older. It's not as easy to stoke the fire in the belly. There's much less joy in getting up at 6 A.M. to catch the early flight to Duluth.

A sense of powerlessness sets in. Frankly, you're at an age where it becomes increasingly difficult to get another job. Logically, a salesperson will look to move laterally—that is to a competitor in the same industry. He knows the products; he knows the customers. What could be better?

The problem with that is after spending twenty or so years pushing his product and her company, it would look more than a little disingenuous to start talking up the very people and products you were talking down the last two decades.

Moving to another industry means starting from the beginning again—learning new products, building a new customer base, forging new relationships. It's not easy at any age.

Still, you are the people I'm writing this book for. Folks who have had good to excellent careers, are not yet ready to retire, but no longer enjoy what they're doing.

Over the last thirty years, I've trained about a half-million sales professionals. I know the animal. I've talked to thousands of sales managers and senior sales and marketing executives. This isn't new. What is new is the changing face of business. When a salesperson hit the wall in the good old days, companies would let him hang on. Let him work his book until he was ready to call it quits.

Companies either can't or won't do that any more. If you're not producing at peak levels . . . well, look at the newspaper any day for reports of white-collar layoffs. This book is intended to show you how to maintain a youthful performance level and, in a worst-case scenario, how to find a job that values your skills.

P A R T

WHERE YOU ARE NOW

1

A Tale from the Front

I got the idea for this book about five years ago at 3 A.M. Or at least that's when the phone rang.

If you've never been woken by a phone call in the middle of the night, you have no idea of the feelings that rage through your body. At first, you're confused. Where am I? Then your heart starts pounding. No one ever calls with good news in the middle of the night. Someone is sick. Someone is dying.

And of course your wife or husband or significant other starts to panic, as well. So while you're fumbling for the phone, she or he starts yelling, "Who is it? What's the matter? Tell me."

In this case, it was a troubled friend, Lew. He apologized for calling so late. He'd dialed my number several times over the preceding weeks but put the phone down before the call went through.

He needed to speak to me but was embarrassed by the subject matter. He hadn't been sleeping lately. He was up and he decided if he didn't screw up his courage to call now he might never do it.

I spent a few more minutes on the phone with him and quickly determined that this was a personal not national emergency that could wait until the next day. Well, actually, later that same day. So I promised

I'd call him first thing and went back to bed. Notice I didn't say I went back to sleep. I just went back to bed.

Let me fill you in on a few details.

Lew and I have been friends since childhood. We grew up in the same neighborhood, went to school together, and played ball together after school. He was a year or two older than me, but we hung out together anyway.

We've stayed in touch all these years, and while we're not as close now as we were then, our families still get together two or three times a year, and Lew and I will have lunch every couple of months.

We've watched each other prosper. Lew has spent his entire career selling technology. He was among the first and most successful copier salespeople and then went into computers. He was offered managerial jobs, but he enjoyed the competitive nature of sales far too much to give it up for a desk. Lew wanted to stay on the front lines. From what I could tell, he had a large and loyal customer base, made good money, and was content with his job particularly and his life in general.

So his call set up enough alarm bells with me that I postponed a lunch with a client—something I never do—and agreed to meet him. Lew was always a happy, upbeat guy. But the guy who walked in was downcast and seemed to have aged years in the couple of months since I'd last seen him. Although I didn't say anything to him about it, Lew suddenly looked more like his father than the friend I remembered.

GETTING OLDER ISN'T EASY

When we were seated at the restaurant, Lew ordered a drink—something he never did at lunchtime—and his story started spilling out.

"What happened to us? What happened to all the plans we had? What happened to all the things we were going to accomplish?"

He went on about the fact that he was closer to retirement than he was to his youth. He realized that in a relatively short period of time, he would lose his identity as Mr. Computer—which is what he called himself. And that he hadn't really done all the things he thought he would have by this time in his life. There were safaris he'd intended to take and marathons he'd wanted to run and countries he wanted to visit, and suddenly he decided that time had passed him by.

At first as I listened to him it sounded "merely" as though he was going through a midlife crisis. I figured I'd suggest he buy a sports car and that would be the end of it. He was only in his early fifties at the time. As far as I was concerned he had more than enough time to safari and travel and run—if not a marathon, at least a 10K. But of course when a person is in the kind of mood that Lew was in, you don't try to talk logically to him. You just sit and listen while he vents.

It turns out that Lew had a new boss, a kid. Or at least he was a kid by Lew's definition. The kid had started a few months earlier and almost immediately started telling Lew all the things that he was doing wrong. Lew had been in sales for three decades or so, and here was this little punk telling him how to sell. A kid who—according to Lew—was still wet behind the ears.

By Lew's second drink, it became clear that there was other stuff bothering him. This kid had upset his apple cart. Lew had grown into a comfort zone at his company. He had a list of happy clients. The money was good. The benefits were great. And the expectation was that he was going to retire from here. Now, unexpectedly, he was afraid he was going to be aged out.

In reality that wasn't going to happen. Lew consistently was a good if not spectacular salesperson. In his worst years he managed to meet his quota, and there were years when he ranked among the company's top road warriors. So why did the kid pick on him? I couldn't give him an answer. Then.

LEW HAD FOUR CHOICES

I thought a lot about it for the next few months. What I decided was that the new manager probably didn't have a lot of sales experience—or management experience for that matter. Someone at some time told him that when he starts a new job he has to come in and exert his authority. So he became a bully. What do bullies do? They pick on the person they perceive as the weakest. And to the kid, the oldest guy there was the weakest. If I had been quicker on my mental feet and been able to figure that out sooner, I would have come up with better answers for Lew. There's only one way to deal with bullies: Come right at them.

But the best I could do at the time was to give Lew what I saw were his limited choices. He could:

- Quit, which was clearly not something he was anxious to do.
- Learn to deal with the manager; adapt to the new guy's sales techniques and ways of doing business.
- Try to go over the manager's head and appeal to his allies in the firm—a tactic that rarely works.
- Make a psychological adjustment and just continue doing what he'd done in the past.

But what was gnawing at Lew (now up to his third drink) was the fear that he might actually be outdated. That the kid was right. That the sales he garnered were not up to the account's potential. And that was what kept him up at night. He was afraid that in his early fifties, it was all over for him. Worse still, we had a mutual friend who was a year younger than Lew who had never been sick a day in his life but died of a heart attack a few months before Lew's call to me.

So even I could see everything that was weighing on him. But at the time I had no real answers for him. He ultimately quit that job and moved to another firm where he was unhappy. He eventually retired far earlier than he'd anticipated and with a good deal less money than he might have had.

Getting older

Lew opened my eyes. What happened to him was going on all around me. I had just been so focused on my sales training courses that I hadn't noticed. But after my lunch with Lew I noticed some of my more mature students voicing similar concerns. They'd probably been doing it for a while. I just hadn't noticed.

So I'd pull them aside on breaks and ask how they were dealing with getting older. I asked their managers for their opinions on the subject. I didn't wait for anyone to complain at my seminars. I raised the issue myself. And I've come up with what I hope will prove a helpful guide that will enable you to avoid the Middle Age Doldrums—or get out if you're already caught them.

Staying sales young is a lot easier than you might imagine.

2

Science Proves My Theory

Something nagged at me as I was writing this book. Everything in it was based upon my observations of thousands and thousands of salespeople. Was that sufficiently valid sample to base a book on? I knew that Lew was not alone about the way he felt. But was my empirical data sufficient cause for a book?

About halfway through the writing my eureka moment came—via newspapers all around the world. Everything I believed was not only scientific fact but was more widespread than I'd imagined.

A study done by a team of researchers at the University of Warwick in England and Dartmouth College in New Hampshire proved that having the middle-aged blahs is perfectly normal. And there's more good news. What was once thought to be a phenomenon of Western culture—that is, the United States and Western Europe—is worldwide. I know it's strange to find comfort in the fact that people all over the world starting their forties feel every bit as miserable as you do. But even though I consider myself a good person, I find comfort in that.

Good news and great news

But that's only the good news. The great news is that it's going to get better. The researchers, economists Andrew Oswald (in England) and David Blanchflower (in the U.S.) discovered that happiness in humans has a U-shape. This means that we are happiest when we are young and grow increasingly unhappy as we age. We hit rock bottom at around forty for women and fifty for men.

It happens slowly, but it does not last. In fact, once we hit bottom we start feeling better. In fact, by the time we hit seventy (assuming you're physically fit) you're "as happy and mentally healthy as a twenty-year-old," Dr. Oswald said. "Perhaps realizing that such feelings are completely normal in midlife might help individuals survive this phase."

A couple of surprises

These results came from a worldwide study of two million people in eighty countries. There were a couple of surprises.

First the results were pretty consistent around the world, with only slight variations.

Even more surprising though was that this U-shaped curve exists at all. Scientists had previously believed that psychological well-being stayed reasonably flat as people aged—ignoring both the obvious and yours truly. There are slight variations. Unhappiness in British women tends to peak later than in Americans; British men peak earlier than we do.

What causes the U-shape happiness curve? That, says Dr. Osborn "is unknown. However one possibility is that individuals learn to adapt their strengths and weaknesses, and in midlife quell their infeasible aspirations."

That, of course, is my theory. At some point we recognize that our youthful ambitions may have been overreaching. We're not going to be the President of the United States and we're not going to be heart surgeons. But in our case we've become pretty good salespeople, and that's fine.

There are other possibilities, of course, but the main point I want to stress from the survey is a continuing theme of this book: The best years of our lives are ahead of us.

When I envisioned this book, I imagined people forty and older as my target audience. This survey hadn't been published yet, but based on my experience I could see a lot of people—peers I grew up with and students I've taught—start to burn out at forty. But what the survey shows—and I've always suspected—is that it's possible to snap out of it. In the midst of all that's going on negatively in your professional life, there is a light at the end of the tunnel. And I'm going to help you get there.

3

Discover Who You Are

There are a couple of observations I've made over the years about salespeople that may surprise you. (Actually, there are more than "a couple," but these two are especially pertinent to our subject.)

The first is that most of us didn't start out intending to go into sales.

Think back to when you were a kid. Did you wake up one morning and tells your parents: "I think I'm going to make sales my life's goal!" Of course not. What youngster does? Most kids want to be firefighters or cops or teachers or nurses— glamorous professions. Even at an early age we somehow knew there was little glamour in selling. We didn't need Arthur Miller's Willie Loman to tell us that.

Besides, what is sales? Does that mean you work in K-Mart selling trinkets or for Boeing selling aircraft? The whole idea of sales is kind of amorphous.

A guy I know in Austin, Texas, sells pipes for a supplier to the oil industry. He's from Milwaukee. He was interested in the oil business, and this is the way the recruiter who came to his campus told him was the best way to get into it. Now, twenty years later, he's still selling pipes, though that has absolutely nothing to do with his background or initial career goals. My personal guess is that he still isn't sure how he fell into sales.

Going with the flow

I know I feel that way. My father was in sales, and I hated sales. It was the last thing I wanted to do. But I got out of school without any clear direction and a liberal arts education that qualified me for . . . gee, I don't know . . . nothing. The help-wanted ads in the paper for college graduates that I applied for mostly put me in either sales positions or training programs that ultimately went into sales. Eventually someone offered me a sales job, and as far as I was concerned it was a temporary position. I took it only because it held the promise that I could make a lot of money quickly. It was never intended to become a career.

Or so I thought.

I was at a point in my life where I felt I better taking *something*, and I went out and started cold calling. I just went with the flow.

I wasn't a verbal Nureyev, but I spoke well. And after a slow start, I got the hang of it. And the more I understood selling, the better I got. And the better I got the more I enjoyed selling. And the more I enjoyed selling, the more successful I became. Selling became a challenge for me. A signed contract wasn't just about commission; it was a victory, another notch on my gun, another medal on my chest. I was never satisfied.

Which leads me to another observation: There are thousands of different products in the world that need to be sold. Yet there are really—in essence—only two kinds of salespeople. There are the kind like the one I became in my mid-twenties—competitive, fire-in-the-belly, won't take no for an answer salespeople. And there are order takers. People content to just get by.

I recently sat next to a salesman executive on a plane, and he used a slightly different terminology. He called them hunters and farmers. Farmers are good at nurturing crops (that is, existing accounts), while hunters go out in the field of cold calling and come back with game to put on the family table.

But these categories are fluid. I know young people who get into sales and are more interested in making out than making money. They're content to just get by so that they can get out of the office at 5 P.M. and start partying by 6. What happens is that at some point in their lives, they settle down, they get married, they have children, and they become adults. Grown up, they become dissatisfied with their professional lot and set out to improve themselves.

(It's important to note here that the easiest way to improve as a salesperson is to take Steve Schiffman's advice, either as a course or in one of his books. End of embarrassing yet meaningful plug.)

THE FIRE GOES OUT

But the opposite happens as well. Starting at about age forty, lethargy begins to set in. There are a number of potential reasons for this, most of which I'll go into later. But they range anywhere from simple boredom—heck, you've been doing the job for two decades or more—to just being tired and not wanting to push your body as much.

Whatever the reason, starting in their forties, a surprisingly high number of hot-to-trot salespeople become content to fox trot their way through work. It doesn't necessarily happen all at once. Sometimes it isn't a conscious decision; it just happens. And sometimes it happens because of the way people look at us now that we're older.

Because you are reading this book, my guess is that you are or were a fire-in-the belly kind of salesperson. Order takers don't bother about change; in fact, they often don't even see the need for it. They continue with their routine, doing the best they can. And they certainly wouldn't invest in a book to help them do what they're doing better, because they don't understand (or care) that there is a better.

So for the purposes of this book, I'm going to address you fire-in-the-belly salespeople. To understand where you are now, it's important to understand where you've been. I've come up with ten traits of successful salespeople, strengths they all have. I bet you recognize your present or former self here. Good salespeople like us are:

1. Not "normal" like everyone else. By normal, of course, I mean, like everyone else, average, vanilla. We're a special breed, bulldogs not Chihuahuas. We're the folks in the Frank Sinatra song, "High Hopes." We will make that sale, and keep coming at a client until we do.

2. Committed to our goals. More than committed, we're obsessed by them. We're also committed to our company's goals, our customers' goals and our own goals—both professional and personal.

3. Self-motivated. We don't need anyone to tell us what to do. We know.

4. Self-declared. That is, we feel pretty good about ourselves; we're comfortable in our skin. We know we're fallible and not everything is going to turn out perfectly. We understand that it's okay to make a mistake.

5. Willing to sacrifice. We've made choices in our lives and live with them.

6. Able to delegate. We don't try to take on the whole world. We prioritize. We know what we're capable of.

7. Optimists. We're part of the solution not the problem. We believe we will close every sale we pursue.

8. Enthusiastic. And our enthusiasm is contagious.

9. We're able to use time wisely. We do little things. For example, we don't schedule client appointments around rush hour.

10. Consistent and persistent. We give the same message to all our customers: I've created a sales program to fit you and your company's needs, not mine. And I keep at it until the client understands we're on the same team.

What happens to these traits as we get older is part of what we'll be discussing over the next several chapters.

4

LOOK IN THE MIRROR

There is an important thing to note early on in this chapter. Getting older by itself does not make you a bad or worse salesperson. In fact, I've met many who improved with age, who were able to use the experience they'd gathered over the years to make the sales process easier for themselves.

But I think they are the exception rather than the rule. For most of us there comes a time when we realize we have—how to put this delicately—matured. That our body can no longer do the things it once did. Moreover, everything that's happened to us is exacerbated by our jobs. Sales is one of the most pressure-filled careers around.

If you're good at it—and I assume you are, because you're reading this book—you always need to be on. You're not an air traffic controller, but you are in a what-have-you-done-for-me-lately business. You're judged by your last sale, by how much you go over quota, your book. It's not an easy life, and studies have shown that this kind of pressure wears you down physically.

And the stress never ends. You might be in the midst of the best year you've ever had in your professional life. All your old customers love you and are placing orders like there's no tomorrow. You've signed up a dozen (no two dozen) new clients and passed your quota months ago. But down deep you know that come January 1, you're back at ground zero. Only this year your quota may be higher.

THE PRESSURE IS UNENDING

And it's not just a function of meeting quota. You're always on: cold-calling people, most of whom won't see you and most of those who do will reject you; lunches and dinners out; the loneliness of life on the road, dealing with late trains and planes. I have this vivid recollection of coming down for dinner in a Holiday Inn in Ottumwa, Iowa, maybe twenty-five or thirty years ago, and seeing twenty other guys just like me, all in tables for one reading newspapers while waiting to be served, acting as though we enjoyed it.

To be honest with you, at the time I did. But I'd run into people who didn't. They'd come up to me at the end of a class or speech and describe their frustration and the all-around blahs they were feeling. I couldn't relate to what they were saying to me. I just saw a bunch of middle-aged guys with spreading waistlines whining about getting older.I thought to myself: cut back on the booze and go to a gym and you'll feel better. Because I didn't understand what they were going through, I'd give them a bromide response and leave it at that. And then it happened to me.

I remember the moment I became old.

It happened of all places in the restroom of a restaurant where my wife and I were dining. Even though I wasn't an employee, I washed my hands. As I did so, I looked in the mirror and suddenly found my father looking back at me. I don't know how it happened, and I don't know why it happened so suddenly, but overnight I'd become my father.

That's when I started noticing things that I'd ignored before. When the doorman at the hotel said, "I'll get you a cab, young man," was he being sarcastic? Or had I just become paranoid?

If we're lucky (consider the alternative), we all have that kind of epiphany at some point. For many it comes when we notice that our sales bags get heavier. For others, it's when a child gets married. Or when we become grandparents. It doesn't happen to everyone at the same time or in the same way, but it does happen to all of us.

The irony is that the moment almost always comes as a shock. It certainly did for me. Until then, I didn't feel a thing. I was as active as I'd always been. I played sports. I attended the theater and movies regularly. I had an active social life. I didn't *feel* old.

But after I noticed my dad in the mirror, I began to see a lot of other things that had changed. When I jogged two days in a row, for example, my time on day two decreased appreciably.

And I found that mentally (more on that in the next chapter) I wasn't nearly as competitive as I once was. I'd been a hunter and seemed to be moving over to farming. My kids had grown. My financial needs had decreased, but the pressure on me to produce increased. Because mine is really a small business, much of its success or failure rested on my shoulders. I have employees with families, many of whom have been with me for a long time. And the pressure, which had never been a problem before, began to weigh heavily against me.

But going the way I had been was an unattractive option. Just the travel alone was knocking me out. Because my clientele is international, it wasn't unusual for me to put on 200,000 air miles a year—in coach. (I'm actually writing this while I'm in Moscow for a week. Then I return to New York for a day before heading out to California. I am sure that in about three weeks when this is all over I will crash.)

Ironically, I used to enjoy traveling and proudly defined myself as a road warrior. So what changed? For one thing, travel in the post-9/11 world has become more difficult. But the more I thought about it—and there was a period when I thought about it a great deal—the more I realized that my older body was having a problem keeping up with my schedule. It's like what happened to me after jogging. It was taking me longer to recover.

And while I was much too young to retire, I was more than ready to cut back on my hours generally and my time on the road specifically. The problem was that when I did cut back, I found I wasn't as happy as I'd hoped I'd be. I realized I'd pulled back for the wrong reasons. It wasn't that I wanted to quit working. It was that I did not know how to cope with the changes that were taking place—in my body and in my mind. No one had ever written a manual before. I briefly went through a classic midlife crisis, and fortunately I figured out some stuff before it was too late.

YOU'RE NOT ALONE

Let me say right up front, I'm not whining. It's important to understand that you're not alone. What you are going through is not unique. It's something I will harp on throughout the book, because if you believe you walk around with a permanent cloud over your head, you'll just wallow in self-pity. And that won't make anything better!

A surprisingly significant amount of my work lately has been with senior (that is in terms of age and experience) salespeople. I've noticed that when I mention the middle age sales crisis, the eyes of ninety percent of the students light up. For many of them it was a lot like having an illness that no doctor seemed able to diagnose. Perhaps they believed they were imagining things. It was a comfort for them to understand that there were other people just like them.

The truth of the matter is that all these changes are probably caused by physiological changes. Women go through menopause, but Gail Sheehy in her book *Passages for Men* says that guys deal with a form of menopause as well. The midlife crisis men go through is every bit as real as those experienced by women. Men (and I'm concentrating on the guys here mostly because the changes in women are more documented) may find that they get depressed more often or mentally fatigued quicker.

But physical changes alone are not the cause of the blahs. There are mental changes as well, and changes in the way you are perceived. We'll be discussing that in the next chapter.

5

MENTAL FATIGUE

A few chapters ago, I mentioned a sales executive I met on a flight. We were crowded into seats on the back of a full plane, and we got to talking. Of course, when I found out that he was a vice president of sales for a large international printing concern and that he had forty people working for him, I—surprise—managed to steer the conversation toward sales training.

As it happens, it was an area of special interest to him. He'd actually begun his professional life as a college geology teacher before switching to sales. His first job was with Xerox (where he stayed for twenty-eight years working his way up the ladder). The interesting thing about Xerox back then, he said, was that it preferred to hire salespeople without experience—and presumably without bad habits.

Xerox preferred to train its people in the Xerox way and then give them time to mature into their jobs. But it doesn't work that way anymore. The age of the benevolent corporation has pretty much ended. You don't have to be a financial analyst to understand that financial pressures on CEOs to keep profits and stock prices high have done away with corporate patience.

Kicking back and relaxing is no longer an option. Kindly sales VPs won't look aside when poor old Bill, who has been with the company for twenty or thirty years, isn't producing the way he used to. Loyalty is extinct.

The irony is that the baby boomer generation—not to mention Generations X and Y—are at or just getting to the age when it could use a little relaxation. We're getting on in years, and at a time when a little relaxation, a little time away from the stress, sounds pretty good.

Again, I am happy to use myself as an example. I recently read the year-end issue of a major glossy magazine that had an "In Memoriam" section. It included a list of all the famous people in show business who died the preceding year. You probably know where I'm going with this. I'd say I was older than forty percent of them, and I am, in the greater scheme of things, still a young man who is years from collecting Social Security, which is my way of telling you I won't say how old I really am.

THERE'S MORE TO LIFE THAN SALES

I don't know if you've ever had the same reaction, but when you start reading things like "In Memoriam" articles, it's understandable that you question yourself and the direction you're heading. Every year it becomes a little more difficult to set the alarm at 6 A.M. Every year it becomes a little more difficult to get in the car and go to work and go out on the sales call. And every year you have more reason not to: grandchildren you want to see, cruises you want to take, a cooking class you want to attend. And if you have a steady stream of income from clients generating sufficient if not extraordinary income for you, it's easy to pull back. It's easy to try to close a deal over the phone rather than visit the client in person.

You may not be ready to retire emotionally or financially, but why not cut back?

But the temptation to cut back is dangerous. The changing economic climate is one factor. Pick up the business section of any newspaper on almost any day and you'll see that another company is cutting back. Layoffs here and there. Additional financing required. Every job is precious.

Back to the guy I met on the plane: his son just got his MBA from the University of Chicago and couldn't find a job. So I don't think relaxing is in the cards. There are people waiting—nay, praying—to take your place.

But besides the financial pressures on your employer you may find that you'll be experiencing financial pressures of your own because the premise on which you based your decision to coast is probably wrong. Those regular checks you expect from long standing clients don't always magically appear.

Depending upon your sales cycle, from one sale to the next a competitor may develop a product that is better, cheaper, or both. Your personal ties with your client can only go so far in protecting your business. The incumbent always starts out with the advantage, but he doesn't always end up with the contract.

The other point is that your buddy at the client's office may not always be there. Clients get promoted, move on to new jobs . . . and get canned.

So cutting back may not be the appropriate response. But is there a way to strike a balance, to use the expertise and wisdom that you've accumulated over the years to have it all? You may not be able to have it all, but you'll certainly have a lot.

6

A Review: Where We've Been and Where We're Going

This might be a good place to pause for a second and review what I've attempted to lay out for you in the first five chapters. First the bad news:

Sales has always been a stress-filled job. But it's become more so in a twenty-first century economic climate where there's constant pressure to increase profits and do more with less. All this weighs on younger people, but it can create particularly strong anxiety among their more mature brethren—folks as young as forty who've been plying the sales trade for two decades or more.

This pressure can affect you physically. Stress breaks down the body's natural immune system, making you more susceptible to illness and depression. At the same time, your old gray body just ain't what it used to be. You're slowing down.

And you're not the only one who recognizes it. The people around you in jobs that used to be held by your peers age-wise are now held by kids, some of them young enough to be your children. And they look at you strangely and engage you differently, as though you're a relic from Discovery Channel's *Dinosaur Week*.

You're not ready to retire, but you have the I-don't-want-to-get-up-at-5 A.M.-to-catch-an-early-morning-flight blahs. So instead of pushing yourself to the limit, you coast on existing accounts that provide you more than enough commissions to meet your needs. This is dangerous, because no company can afford to keep someone on staff—in any position—who just coasts.

Now that I've thoroughly depressed you—and, frankly, I'm not in that good a mood myself—let me tell you the good news.

Not everyone goes through the *Sturm und Drang* I've just described in terms of work. Some people have crises at home in terms of personal relationships that never impact them at work. When it comes to sales, these people are genetically gifted. They're slim and trim and youthful. They thrive on challenges and stress. And for those few of you who fit into this category and are reading this book, I have a couple of quick points to make:

- I hate you.
- You don't have to read any further; but having read up to Chapter 6, it's too late to return this book to the bookstore.
- For the rest of us, the good news is that none of the problems I've discussed are fatal—particularly if you don't want them to be. You can come back as a relic of Discovery Channel—but from Shark Week. It is easy to reclaim your inner shark.

The thing to remember is that we're going to tackle a number of different issues. Some of them might strike comparatively close to home. Some of them may be on topics that don't concern you—yet. Read them anyway. You never know when one of these things might pop up again.

First, the young sales manager.

GROWING OLDER
Elie Wiesel

Elie Wiesel is a Holocaust survivor who went on to win the Nobel Peace Prize for his work to keep the memory of the Holocaust alive and prevent its repetition.

Like everybody else, I like old people but not old age. In antiquity, old age was a curse. We all want to be old and young at the same time. Longevity is not a popular word. We prefer to speak of senior citizens or golden age.

In truth, society is not too kind toward its old men and women. Only the young are of interest to opinion makers and fashion shapers. Youth is a cult with our entire industry worshiping its idols. We owe them allegiance and adoration.

What a strange paradox: On the one hand, medicine is performing miracles to prolong life—but society prevents its benefactors from enjoying it. The old people—we do not know what to do with them. Why don't they stay home? At best, we send them to Florida or Arizona. Victims of mandatory retirement, they must feel useless—and surely ashamed of not being young anymore.

Once upon a time, things were different. Filled with experience, learning, and memory, an old person inspired respect, obedience, admiration, and gratitude. Old age and wisdom were synonymous. A wise person was old and ancient. In those times it was an honor to be old. An eighteen-century philosopher said, "I love all that is old—old wine, old friends, and old books." I would add: old faces. In Rome's Senate, it was always the old who were heard. In Talmudic academies, the old person was always at the center. He was the source of authority.

Well—a society may be judged by its attitude toward the old. Scripture insists on the respect we owe the old. I am supposed to stand up before him. And it is standing that I must listen to his or her words. Their knowledge is *a priori* superior to mine. Their generation is closer to the source than mine. An old man knows more than I because he remembers more events. Thus to work on his behalf is more than an obligation; it is a privilege. To help the helpless is one of our fundamental ethical principles. That applies especially to old people.

Naturally we are duty-bound to help children and adolescents—and their parents. But in their case, we may almost take it as a sound investment. One day the child will grow and become wealthy, wise, learned, and influential—and thus able to pay us back for our faith in his or her future. But helping an old person implies no reward. There it is simply a matter of selfless generosity and grace.

Hence the question: Why does our society do so much for the young and not enough for the old? Why don't we understand that it is our obligation to help the young because they are young and the old because they are not? In the young we celebrate promise, in the old we honor memory. Don't we need both to fulfill ourselves as human beings?

P A R T

HOW TO WIN OVER YOUNGER MANAGERS AND CLIENTS

7

Working with the Young'uns—It's a Matterof Knowing Your Customer

I discussed this book with a close friend who told me a story he finds extremely funny—in retrospect. Actually, "funny" might not be the correct word; it's really more ironic. Almost proof positive that what goes around comes around.

He was about twenty-six the first time he was promoted into a position where he had to hire someone. In essence, he had to find someone to replace himself. He placed an ad in the Sunday paper (this was well before the age of Monster.com) and was almost immediately flooded with over 100 replies. Remember now, he was very young and as he admits now, a little unsure of himself.

This was sometime in the early 1970s, and what he did was interesting. He listened to the Rolling Stones or Bob Dylan or Timothy Leary or whoever it was who said, "Never trust anyone over thirty." He went through the resumes and immediately eliminated those applicants whose resumes indicated they were three or four years (or more) older than he was at the time.

He chuckles about it now, but still vividly remembers the management agony he went through in the process, because even then he understood that his decision reflected his shortcomings, not the short-comings of the people he eliminated.

And now, in what he considers the height of karma coming back to bite him in the, uh, arm, he has applied for positions he knows he can do with his hands tied behind his back. Blindfolded. Submerged in an ice-cold pool of water. But he doesn't get hired because (in his opinion) there is some little pipsqueak MBA somewhere, aware of his shortcomings and a little unsure of himself, who threw my friend's resume in the trash the way he threw the resumes of older people three decades ago.

"I've been around a while," my friend says. "In some instances, I know the people who were hired for jobs that I couldn't get an interview for. And frankly—and clearly I'm not going to be falsely modest here—I'm much better than they are. I know what base they were paying. I have a rough idea of what the quotas were. And as far as I was concerned, the company had a shot at hiring a NASCAR racer and went with a Chevette."

As we baby boomers get older, we're going to run into situations like this all the time. The guys we grew up in the business with, the role models we followed, have or soon will retire. And all of a sudden, we'll be the old guys. Working with—and for—kids young enough to be our children.

WILL A NEW BOSS MINE OUR WISDOM?

Some of them will be smart and look to see if they can profit from the wisdom we've accumulated. But others will automatically assume we're dinosaurs and ought to be out to pasture or whatever they do with dinosaurs now.

I mention this because there's always been tension and misunderstandings between generations. If you're close to me in age (again, we don't have to get specific, but let's say you were born in the decades immediately following World War II) you'll likely remember how our parents railed against Elvis and rock 'n' roll. It was the devil's music. It is much the same way I currently describe hip-hop—meaning of course that the more things change, the more they stay the same.

But there are significant differences, as well. And it's how you deal with those differences that largely will determine how happy you will be. Because, at some point, one of those youngsters will become your boss. And a whole bunch of them will become your clients. I'll deal with both of these subjects in upcoming chapters, but here I'd like to talk to you about something that's common to both situations.

YOU VERSUS THE YOUNGSTERS

There's no sense whining about any of this since the ball is in your court. One of the great things about sales is that you're the one they turn to when they want someone to "show me the money." Even the most insecure, pig-headed, newly promoted, knows-nothing-about-sales-or-marketing executive understands that it's you who brings in the bucks.

The same holds true with the youngster hired by your client to oversee purchasing your product or service. No new kid on the block wants to start off by making waves. My point is that meeting both the new and younger boss and the new and younger client is a lot like a cold call. Something you are, of course, great at.

In making that first impression, it's important to recognize a couple of basic differences between the young people you are likely to meet today and yourself when you were younger. When I first started teaching, for example, my audiences tended to be my age or a little older. That meant it was easy for me to relate to them. Away from the office, we probably watched the same television shows—there were far fewer choices then—went to the same movies, and read the same books.

Younger people today have more discretionary choices that we ever did. We live in a multichannel universe and in the age of the Internet. This is a generalization, I know, but for the most part, younger people don't read books—and when they do it's typically not for pleasure, the way many of us did. This is not intended as a criticism; perhaps if we'd had as many choices as they have, we would not have read either.

A by-product of this is that youngsters—and by youngsters, I mean young people in their twenties and thirties—seem to have a shorter attention span. I've modified all my training classes because of this, shortened each of the modules and added more visual elements. I've done much the same when I make a presentation to a new client.

In the end, all I really did was that I paid attention to my customers' needs. And isn't that what sales is really all about? I used my experience and knowledge to become a better salesperson. And isn't that exactly what this book is about?

Any kind of a sales job is difficult and pressure-filled. It's easy to understand why someone might want to cut back, to coast on past glories. Dealing with younger people—as boss and client—who don't have your depth of experience can certainly be frustrating.

But we have something no kid has—wisdom based on years of experience. And if we use that wisdom wisely (sort of a pun, sort of intended) we can make these years the best of our professional and personal lives.

8

THE NEW YOUNG
SALES MANAGER

When management changes, everyone gets a little nervous. New management means change, and change takes you out of your comfort zone. It's a natural reaction—especially if you're a worrier (as I am). You start to wonder what the new powers that be will be like. If they've been promoted from within, you worry about any slights you may have committed while you were both professional equals. If they've been brought in from the outside, you worry about what new systems they'll introduce, what people they'll bring with them.

And the older you are, the more potential for trouble you see. There really is no way to sugarcoat this. There is a certain amount of prejudice against older people in this country—and by that I mean the true definition of prejudice: to pre-judge.

Despite federal and state regulations, despite the politically correct talk about how bad ageism is, the truth is that older folks are sometimes, often, always (pick any one you like) pre-judged. The assumption is they are no longer hip. When they talk about MySpace, they mean that particular section on the sofa where they always sit to watch TV. Text messaging is as foreign to them as smoke signals. I'm not saying that's necessarily true, but I think it often is the mental picture of older folks many people have.

So it's understandable if some of the older folks on staff are a bit more concerned about new management than some of the younger ones. And the situation is worse when the new manager is young. In fact, the younger he is, the greater the disparity in your ages, the greater the intimidation factor. (A twenty-five-year-old might consider someone over forty-five old. Remember my friend, who didn't trust anyone over thirty.)

A few words about this kind of prejudice. We all do it. Chances are you'll be quick to pre-judge the youthful new manager, a freshly minted MBA with little or no sales experience—especially when put up against your years of wisdom. It's all a matter of perspective.

Don't hate them because they're young

When new management comes in, it's always a little more troubling for the older people on staff. Whether they admit it or not, I'm willing to bet they all spend a little time worrying if their new boss will accept them for what they are and what they've accomplished or judge them based on preconceived notions.

Of course, some people don't have to worry. If you are one of you're company's top salespeople, you are Eliot Ness—that is Untouchable.

If you're not Ness-like, if you've been coasting, the situation is of course different. But not every circumstance is the same. For example, a great deal depends on why the new manager is there. Was the older manager promoted? Did she leave for a better job? Are things going well at the company, or is the suspicion that the new guy was brought in to clean house?

In one respect it doesn't make a difference. No matter the sales manager's mission or perspective on anything—on you, on your talents and abilities—he's there with only one goal in mind, and that is to improve sales. That's the same reason you're there. So, for the moment, anyway, you and the new manager are allies. That's important to keep in mind, because despite the many concerns you have, it's important to believe that gray skies are gonna clear up; so put on a happy, positive face. As far as you're concerned, the new manager means new opportunities. And in some cases that's actually true.

Sadly, there are no one-size-fits-all rules I can offer that work for everyone in every case. Many of my suggestions apply to people of all ages in all situations, not just older salespeople. But they do work.

Be yourself. Don't try to relate to them as though you are the same age. You're not, and to try to act otherwise makes you look foolish. You don't have to quote Fiddy's song lyrics—by the way, that's what those of us in the know call rapper 50 Cent. There's no need to discuss the latest Grand Theft Auto video game. Be who you are.

Play to your strengths. You're strength isn't your knowledge of hip-hop lyrics. Your strength is your experience, your depth of knowledge, and your close relationship with your accounts.

You may have it, but don't flaunt it. Even if you believe the new boss just got out of diapers, don't talk down to her. To say, "I've been selling this way for thirty years," is not a proper response to a new sales manager's suggestions.

Anxiety is a two-way street. Remember, the manager is probably a little nervous. She's in an awkward situation, too. The better your sales, the more she needs you happy. She can't afford to have you quit even if your sales are in the middle of the pack. A new (and smart) manager doesn't want to rock the boat in any way right away. It doesn't look good to senior execs when a new manager's most experienced salespeople quit or become disgruntled. That doesn't reflect well on the new boss. Also, the new manager needs your production, whatever it is. She is under pressure to maintain quotas, and your production is likely to be much higher than a new hire brought in from the outside.

Most sales reps tell me that they want their managers to be honest and forthright in their criticisms. And the managers tell me the same thing.

But each side sometimes means different things. Both of you—manager and sales rep—need to speak the same language. The easiest way to do that is to avoid jargon or two dollar words. A fancy vocabulary is as likely to confuse as to impress.

This, too, shall pass! In the best of circumstances, the new manager, no matter her age, is smart and knows what she's doing. In the worst-case scenario, she's immature, insecure, and caught up with herself. The temptation at some point is to just get up and yell, "Jerk! What don't you understand?" Clearly, that's not the wisest tactic. Bite your tongue. Hold on. Because if she's that much of a jerk she'll soon be gone.

9

Dealing With the
Younger Customer

Customer relationships are difficult under any circumstances. There's a fine line salespeople walk between having a strictly business relationship (which is cold) and a personal relationship (which is rare). The problem is that it's not always clear exactly where that line is. It seems fluid, changing each day (according to the mood of the customer), and from customer to customer.

I remember when I first started in sales. I actually felt a little uncomfortable when the conversation with clients strayed too far into the personal area. I had my speech all mapped out, and discovering that his kids need braces or that her daughter was getting married made me more than a little tense. In the back of my mind I was a little suspicious that gee, was he asking for a kickback, or did she expect me to send a gift?

I probably was being paranoid. But I just didn't have the experience to know how to handle that. And it took some time for me to master that art. This whole business/personal relationship is a regular subject of seminars I conduct. There are a lot of restrictions you have in business conversations that you don't have in personal discussions.

That's obvious—or at least it seems obvious to me. Now. But that goes back to a point I've been trying to make in pretty much every chapter. The chances are that all the experience you have—all the years, you have—has made you a better salesperson, and any concerns you may have about it are ill founded.

Still, all this becomes more difficult when you are suddenly faced with a new person at an established client or you are trying to sell to a prospect and have to deal with a snot-nosed kid. Allow me to please set some parameters to what I mean.

THE PROBLEMS ARE REAL

Not all younger customers will disrespect you. They won't all assume that because the chimney is gray the fire in the belly is out. But some will, only adding to the general malaise and discomfort you may already feel at dealing with a kid.

This very topic came up at one of my seminars a couple of years ago. It was attended by a group of senior sales executives—and by senior I don't mean in job title. There were fourteen people. All of them had at least two decades experience, and their ages ranged from forty-two to sixty-one. We were supposed to be talking about how you make the transition when a long-standing client brings in a new buyer.

I believe it is one of the most difficult things to do in sales. In some ways it's very similar to what we just discussed in the last chapter, in terms of when you suddenly get a new supervisor. We're all creatures of habit. None of us likes change. But when it concerns our livelihoods, we become even more apprehensive.

In the middle of our discussion, one of the salespeople mentioned that he was having a lot of problems with a long-standing client. He'd sold medical equipment to a large privately held company and developed what he thought was an outstanding relationship with his counterpart at the firm. It had started out as a small but steady source of income for him, but over the years he'd nurtured it and it has become one of his two largest accounts.

The salesman's contact retired and a new buyer was brought in from outside the firm. He was a relatively recent MBA, without much experience in the industry, in purchasing, or in sales. But he was making the salesman jump through all kinds of hoops, come up with all kinds of (in the salesman's opinion) needless facts and stats and new price quotes. The salesman who brought the subject up had over twenty-five years selling experience and had serviced this account for nearly fifteen years.

What he said opened the floodgates. All the other participants in the seminar—men and women—came forth with horror stories of their own. And what we came up with then and what I've found in subsequent research is that there is no clear-cut pattern. It is a mistake when you first meet a baby buyer—and I clearly do not mean someone who purchases babies, but an extremely youthful client—to assume that he or she doesn't know what they're doing. Give them benefit of the doubt.

As the Bible says, do unto others as you would have them do unto you. You don't want to be judged by the gray in your hair, so you shouldn't prejudge the kid.

There are a number of important things to remember.

First of all, whether or not the new buyer has been promoted from within or brought in from outside the company, he or she needs to make a good impression, too. They want to impress you with their professionalism and they want to impress their new bosses with their thoroughness. So what you see as a buyer playing let-me-show-you-who's-the-boss mind games is more likely to be thought of by him as just doing his job. Keep in mind that with any degree of luck this, too, shall pass. At some point, the buyer is likely to feel more comfortable behind his new desk and more comfortable trusting you.

Second, the kid may be right. Consider the possibility that you may have become complacent. It happens. Perhaps you've been cruising on this account, and it's time for you to get your head back in the game.

Third, you need to ask yourself what image you are projecting. If you run into someone who rolls his eyes when you make a suggestion and makes it clears he thinks you're a dinosaur—well, could it actually be your fault? Do you carry yourself as an expert? I know this will sound so basic and silly that it need not be said, but haven't we all seen salespeople whose suits need pressing and shoes need shining and hardly project the image of professionalism. It may be time to reinvent yourself—a subject we'll discuss in the next chapters.

In the meantime, here are some suggestions on how to deal with the youthful buyer.

MAINTAIN YOUR SENSE OF HUMOR

You've been doing this for a long time, and the odds are you're not suddenly going to fail now. The truth is that ninety-nine percent of us sell commodities—where comparable products are available from numerous suppliers. (I know you're not going to like the next couple of sentences any more than I enjoy typing them, but the truth must win out.) So it is incumbent upon us to be likable, and likability in sales sometimes means you have to take a certain amount of crap from someone. Sorry.

LIMIT THE B.S.

There is a limit to how much crap you have to take. The best way to deal with a bully is to sock him in the nose. Before I tell you this next story, which illustrates my point, allow me to confess that I did not see all the events that transpired. But I saw enough. I was in the parking garage at LaGuardia Airport in New York City where I observed a guy in a chauffeur's uniform briskly walk away from a guy carrying a couple of pieces of luggage. The guy chasing after the driver was yelling at him, "You have to take me in! It's your job! You're supposed to carry my bags—that's what you get paid for!"

From that brief exchange, I used my Sherlock Holmes deductive reasoning to surmise that the chauffeur had been sent to the airport to pick up the gentleman. The arriving passenger probably had some kind of business relationship with the company that employed the driver. As they were walking toward where the driver had parked his limousine, the guy, who had clearly just arrived on a flight, continued to yell at the driver, saying (and I remember this though it happened a long time ago),

"You damn well better take me in!" The driver ignored him and walked to the car and got in and started to back out of the spot, and all of a sudden the guy's tone changed. He apologized if he was rude and literally begged the driver to let him in the car—to no avail. I'm not sure what started the argument. Maybe the guy just had an attitude—the way a young purchasing agent might. But whatever the problem was, the bully changed his tune when the driver stood up to him. Yes, as I said a couple of paragraphs ago, taking crap is part of the human condition. But so is having a little bit of dignity. Stand up for yourself.

THE ODDS ARE IN YOUR FAVOR

Statistically, you have a better chance of getting additional business from an existing account than another supplier coming in from the outside. Similarly, the odds are you're going to keep this business. It's a hassle for the new person to come in and upset an apple cart that's in perfect working order. It's a hassle for the buyer to have to go through the rigmarole of finding another supplier.

USE YOUR ALLIES

Presumably you've built a retinue of contacts and friends within the company. They may be willing to help with any problems you encounter.

HELP THE GUY DO HIS JOB

Before you start a feud, try to get on his side. (I keep using masculine pronouns, because in all my years in the business I've only run into one woman executive who liked to throw her weight around just for the sake of throwing her weight around. By way of contrast, I've had to work with a couple of dozen male execs who had ego problems and liked to use their underlings as punching bags.) Show him you can be a valuable ally.

You can always punt!

If everything fails, if you can't get the guy to like you and win back the business, do what I do. Prospect! Don't grovel. Don't beg. Get new business. I don't mean to minimize the impact losing this account might have on your income and your ego. But this is not likely to be the first account you've lost. And even though it may not be deserved, you have to get past it and move on. You know what they say: "Don't get mad. Get new accounts."

I have that right, don't I?

10

THINGS TO PUT ON
YOUR TO DON'T LIST

I am currently the youngest-looking and youngest-thinking guy I went to school with. I was unaware of this until I recently attended my college reunion. I cannot begin to tell you how everyone else has aged.

I, on the other hand, have managed to remain youthful in body and spirit. Sure I've successfully added several years chronologically (I say successfully by comparison to the alternative), but mentally and in large measure physically I'm still a kid. If you listen to my wife, I've also stayed emotionally immature, but that's another story.

My point is that I still *believe* I'm young, and while believing or wishing won't make it so, it is a positive step. A friend of mine in the clothing business sells fine men's wear, tailored suits and the like. He advertises in *The Robb Report, Departures,* and *GQ,* among other upscale publications. The models he shows, though, are all young and hardly the kind of people likely to purchase one of his suits.

I asked him about it. I said none of the models in the ads look like me. And he responded that that was the point. He wants the ad to make me and people like me feel as though they could look like those skinny models, if only they bought his suits. I understand that ain't gonna happen, but I really would like to look that good, because in my mind's eye, that's pretty much what I look like.

On the other hand, if you think old, you'll act old. I have in the preceding chapters made a number of suggestions about what you can and should do to stay youthful (or at least youthful-like). Here are additional things you should do.

GET RID OF THE SNEAKERS AND JEANS AT WORK

I know it's fashionable now to dress down. I know a lot of companies have casual dress workdays. I know the cool thing is to wear sneakers, jeans, and a sports jacket. And that may be all right if you work in some creative area. Let's say you're a filmmaker or a radio disk jockey. Or perhaps you're the art director at a large international advertising agency.

However, if you are reading this book, my guess is that you are not any of those things. You are a salesperson. So it is important that you dress appropriately for your position. A salesperson needs, among other things, to look professional. One of the mantras I tell my students is that you only get one chance to make a first impression. You always need to be dressed as though you're visiting your most conservative client. If what you are wearing might turn him or her off, don't wear it!

That's true for any salesperson, but even more so for someone of—how to put this tenderly—advanced years. Wear tight jeans and flowered Hawaiian shirts and you can come off looking like an aging hippie who thinks we're still in the sixties. Stop wearing that big chain around your neck that you thought made you look cool. Now it makes you look stupid. The Rat Pack is dead. You'll likely become an object of ridicule rather than respect. And while I'm at it, may I also suggest that you get rid of the backpack? You're dressed in a suit going to a sales meeting, not climbing a mountain. A good briefcase leaves a better impression and doesn't drag down your right shoulder while you walk.

DRESS PROFESSIONALLY

There is no excuse to dress down, not even the weather. A salesman came to see me a couple of summers ago on a hot New York City afternoon. He was an older guy—and by older I mean my age. He came in with his sleeves rolled up, carrying his jacket and holding a bottle of water. It was boiling out, but my office isn't in the Sahara. I felt frankly as though we were going to sit down and play cards, not have a sales meeting. To this day I don't have any idea what he was thinking. I didn't buy anything from him, in part because of his slovenly appearance. But, also, because his appearance translated into the way he conducted the entire sales call—as sloppy as his dress.

By way of contrast, I used to have a salesperson who worked for me who perspired as though he was in a sauna. On a typical summer day when he'd come in from an appointment he'd literally drip on some of the paperwork. But he was conscientious and knew the importance of a professional appearance. So on hot days he'd get to appointments early and either sit in the lobby or go to the building coffee shop for a soda or iced tea and the opportunity to cool down.

You have to dress appropriately for your age. That doesn't mean you have to wear your pants up to your chest, but it does mean no baseball caps.

STOP TALKING ABOUT THE GOOD OLD DAYS

No one wants to know that you played minor league football or baseball. It's great that you were a celebrity in high school. But unless you're Bruce Springsteen, people don't want to hear about your glory days. They also don't want to know how you sold when selling was really selling, not the baby stuff they do today. No one wants to hear your war stories. Stop being a bore!

I recently conducted a sales seminar attended by a dozen sales reps. There was one woman there who had maybe six or seven years experience. But for the other eleven attendees, this was their first job out of college. Somehow—I don't remember exactly under what circumstances—the song "Begin the Beguine" came up. No one—let me note that again—*no one* had ever heard of it. And only two or three of them had ever heard of the song's composer, Cole Porter.

I was flabbergasted. I mention this because it reinforces a couple of points I want to make. I've spoken about the wisdom that we as older, more experienced salespeople have—not only about sales but life. I want to add something to that. Somehow it seems to me we're just generally smarter than the younger generation.

Perhaps that's because we didn't have as many distractions when we were growing up. When I was a child, Uncle Miltie was getting people to buy their first TVs. I grew up in New York and there were seven channels. In other parts of the country, there weren't even that many. Now we're talking about 500 channels, text messaging, and video games. Who has time to read?

So if you get a little depressed by the young'uns, remember that you are so much better than they are. You know so much more and are capable of doing so much more than they ever dreamed of. That should give you strength. But don't let them know how smug you are.

I must have spent a minute or so marveling at the fact that they didn't know the song. "You don't know 'Begin the Beguine'? That's part of the American songbook. How could you not know that?" Then I saw their eyes glaze over. Largely I believe because they didn't understand the significance of the American songbook to our culture, they could care less about the song or that they'd never heard of it. Who cares? Did Cole Porter have an East Coast feud with the Gershwins? Did 50 Cent ever sample a Cole Porter ditty? Then who cares?

So I quickly stopped my self-satisfied, boy-am-I-superior rant and moved on. The good old days are over. Deal with the new realities.

Bring Your Photo Album Up to Date

In a related "don't," bring the photos in your office or cubicle into the twenty-first century. No one wants to see pictures of you playing golf in 1963. Why have reminders around for your coworkers to see how old you really are? Why give them a chance to say, "Harry, did people really dress like that?"

Don't Overcompensate with Your Language

There's no need to speak hip-hop. Can you feel me? While it looks funny in the movies when some older guy tries to be hip, in real life it's often pathetic. People see right through it. If you want to have a discussion, have it on your terms. Don't be afraid to be the intellectual. Ultimately you'll be admired for it.

Don't be patronizing

One of the things I remember from when I first started is that I had a manager who had this incredibly annoying way of talking down to me. I resented him and still do. On the other hand, I had a manager who understood the need to be disciplined in your work, and he conveyed it in a way that was both easily understandable and not at all patronizing. The analogy isn't perfect, but you understand the point. Don't come off as superior.

Get comfortable in your Skin—or shed it slowly

A guy I knew—a smart person who owned a retail chain—came into his office one day with the blackest hair I've ever seen. Up until that point, he was salt and pepper gray and quite distinguished looking gentleman. My guess is that he woke up one day, looked in the mirror and suddenly realized he was mature. So he dyed his hair. He looked silly when he came in because he was overcompensating to the point where he looked unnatural.

I'm reminded of the famous line Gerry Ford said during a campaign about Ronald Reagan: "He doesn't dye his hair. He's just prematurely orange."

Or what about the famous Giuliani combover?

Did you ever see a guy with a really bad and obvious wig? I always wonder what he's thinking when he looks in the mirror. Does he tell himself, "Hey, this is a good look"?

Let it go. Or, if you feel the need to make changes, at least make them subtle. Spend the extra bucks and make changes gradually, over time.

Don't confuse business and personal relationships

The two are completely different. That you are invited to go out for drinks with the rest of the sales team is not a sign that your younger boss wants to go to a ball game or the theater with you. That you treat a younger customer to an expensive lunch doesn't mean she wants to get together with you and your family for a picnic. Stay professional.

GROWING OLDER
BERT VOGELSTEIN

Bert Vogelstein is a noted cancer researcher who led the team that discovered the specific mutations responsible for cancer of the colon, a dramatic breakthrough in our understanding of the genetic basis of cancer.

Age has indeed affected the way I do "business."

As I have gotten older, I have realized that I will never be able to accomplish all the goals that I thought might be possible when I was younger.

This has forced me to focus on those goals that I think are most important and realistic. This focus has had positive ramifications both for me and the younger people I work with.

PART

USE YOUR EXPERIENCE

11

SELLING THE WAY YOU SOLD WHEN YOU WERE YOUNG

Do you remember when you were in third or fourth grade and you learned cursive writing? It was a major step forward from printing, but your penmanship had to be just so. Every curlicue had to be positioned just so, every "i" dotted and every "t" crossed.

Take a look at your handwriting now. Do you even have curlicues? Frankly it has gotten so bad that *I* can't even read my handwriting.

Another example is when I first learned how to drive—especially when my dad was in the car giving me lessons. I would—to use the penmanship example again—dot every "i" and cross every "t." I'd never go over the speed limit. I'd triple check the mirrors before changing lanes. In the years since then, I've come to realize that a yellow light means speed up and the speed limits signs are more guidelines that actual rules.

What tends to happen the older and more experienced we become is that we drift away from the basics and kind of mold the rules to a way that works for us. When it comes to sales, for example, perhaps the rule when you came up was to spend an hour a day prospecting. Then you built up a client list, so perhaps you spent a half hour a day prospecting and then fifteen minutes daily and then fifteen minutes every other day.

Perhaps you used to make up detailed and personalized presentations, but found it was easier to do a one-size-fits-all production.

You can see where I'm going with this. You're caught somewhere between the blahs and extreme pressure to produce. But you've been doing things one way so long you don't know where to begin. The answer is really simple: go back to basics. To me it's like a team manager going into the World Series or Super Bowl with a clean up hitter or quarterback who's hit a rough patch. Does he substitute for the player going through a slump or trust the guy who brought him to the Big Game? I think most managers agree that you dance with the guy who brought you to the ball.

BACK TO BASICS

It's the same with you and me. If you want to recapture your success, you have to go back to the techniques that made you successful in the first place. Maybe you have to sit down and re-read (my) sales books. Or sign up for (my) sales training courses. In upcoming chapters, we're going to talk more about the specifics of the selling process to help jog your memory. But when I say you need to go back to basics, I don't mean just the details of selling. You have to recapture the enthusiasm of your youth.

I hate the term "fire in the belly." It sounds like someone needs an antacid. But while I dislike that expression, you clearly know what I mean. There was this time in your life when it seemed everything you wanted was within your grasp. Do you remember when the excitement of selling was enough to get you up in the morning? When each new day represented a series of new challenges?

But after awhile, after the four hundredth trip to the same client who wants another modification of your contract worth about $100 a month, you start to wear down. Remember that fire in your belly? When you burn out, you extinguish it. But the very fact that you've bought and are reading this book means you want to get back to your winning ways. You want to reinvent yourself. Ironically, I was very young when I had that kind of epiphany.

Hiding from the job

I'd only been selling a couple of years, and quite frankly I was hawking a very crappy product. On a very nasty, rainy day in New York City I just decided to go to the movies. (And before you start smirking, no, it wasn't one of those movies.) It was the middle of the workweek. I figured no one would know, and that I'd probably be the only one in the theater.

So here I am, this twenty-five-year-old kid with my sales bag walking into a darkened theater—and I have trouble finding a seat. The place is packed with other salespeople, who are tired and wet and getting out of the rain. To me, looking at them from the vantage point of my youth, all I saw was losers. And then it occurred to me that *I was one of them!* I was a loser, hiding from my job. Really, I was hiding from my future.

I told myself that I wouldn't let that happen to me. That evening I sat down and made a career plan for myself. I sat down with a pencil and paper and created a Master Plan and timeline: what I wanted to accomplish, what my timeframe was, and how I was going to do it. Things didn't work out exactly the way I'd planned. But I did come very close to my overall objectives. And while my life's graph isn't one steady line up, while I've faltered occasionally, I pretty much did keep to the spirit of that plan.

I don't know what your epiphany was, what moment of truth prompted you to reevaluate your career. Perhaps it was that new, young manager looking at you askance. Maybe it was doing your taxes and realizing that your income over the last five years was flat or down while your expenses were up.

It doesn't make a difference. The fact that you've had your epiphany and want change is really all that matters. So what's the next step?

Make a plan

It may not be for everyone, but sitting down and writing out a plan, stating my objectives, putting them into the context of a timeframe worked for me. Why? Because it forced me to think about where I was in my life and how far that was from where I wanted to be. And just thinking about it created a sense of urgency.

Essentially, reinventing or reinvigorating yourself is a two-step process. The first involved getting back to basics. Certainly you remember most of it, but it doesn't hurt to take a refresher course. I don't like the word "training." My daughter has a golden Labrador retriever, and the dog has been trained.

You're in sales. You don't need to be taught to sit or beg or shake paws. You need to be reminded about the sales process and figure out how to best use it in your circumstances. You may need a wakeup call on what I consider the three basic elements of sales: prospecting, presenting, and explaining your product.

The Kid May Know What She's Doing, After All

But I've long felt that harking back to the way you sold when you were young(er) is the easy part—like getting on a bicycle after not riding for a while. I'll be discussing the basic elements of the sales process, in upcoming chapters. But first I'd like to talk to you a little about recapturing your youthful enthusiasm.

I was with my daughter (the one who owns the golden Labrador retriever) a few weeks before I completed this chapter, and I had another epiphany. We were discussing politics, and I suddenly realized she knew more about the subject under discussion than I did. And for the first time I listened. She had insights that amazed me. Within a matter of minutes, the parent/child relationship we'd had was thrown on its ears. Teaching wasn't a one-way street any more. It turns out that there was a lot I could learn from her.

I hired a young man, a few yeas ago. My initial plan was to use him as a kind of glorified gofer. But in a matter of weeks he infected me with his enthusiasm for the job, an excitement that I'd forgotten. You have that opportunity, too.

The Career Salesperson

I hope that I didn't paint too bleak a picture, a kind of us (older guys) vs. them (younger guys) mentality. (And lest there be any question, I mean men guys and women guys.) It's not that at all. The demon you're fighting is largely inside you. Sure, there are younger people—both managers and clients—who may assume that you are over the hill. But that doesn't mean you have to accept their assumption as truth—because we all know what happens when we assume.

Over the course of my career I've had a couple of important mentors—older, more experienced salespeople—who helped teach me the ropes, who nurtured me. But you know what? My role models now are younger people. They have vitality. It's one of the reasons I always suggest that an older salesperson take on the role of mentor, to help guide youngsters. As an aside, I think this is especially important role for experienced women to take on, because despite all the advances we've made in terms of feminism, women still don't have a sufficient number of good role models in sales.

My experience is that when you mentor you learn as much as you teach. The question is: How do you make yourself comfortable hanging around with a younger person? The answer: It's in the next chapter.

12

REFRESH YOURSELF

I am not Dr. Phil. But I have been around sales long enough and worked with enough salespeople—about 500,000 by my count—to have noticed a couple of things that are common to all of us.

I suspect it's because of the constant pressure particular to our business, but a lot of us go through a series of mini-crises as we get older. It's not just the younger bosses and customers we encounter. And it's not just the blahs or a desire to cut back and coast. It's all of these things. Truth be told, I've gone through it myself a bunch of times. And when I do, I've come to understand it's time to refresh and renew myself.

What do I mean by refresh and renew? We all become set in our ways. We get used to doing things in a certain way and become resistant to anything new. So you have to shake things up, physically, mentally, and professionally. Force yourself to look at yourself and life differently.

This chapter's theme is that you owe it to yourself to take care of you. If you do that, if you concentrate on all the positive attributes you bring to the workplace, you will develop a better attitude and that will most assuredly translate into higher sales. And it all starts with taking better care of your body.

Shaking Things Up Physically

Sadly there are times when you look in the mirror and it's hard not to get down on yourself. They don't call it middle age spread for nothing. It sort of sneaks up on you—and suddenly you're your father. One day you're thin and trim, and then you have to take deeper and deeper breaths to get into your pants.

Image isn't everything in sales, but it does count for a lot. If you are overweight and appear slovenly—I'm sorry, but I couldn't think of a better word—it will affect the way you are perceived in the same way as being older can impact people's perception of you. And it will likely affect your self-esteem.

Obviously, you need to figure out an exercise regimen. You don't have to be Dr. Phil to know that. I know—from personal experience—that that's easier said than done. You don't have to be Dr. Phil to know that, either. But several important things will happen if you begin an exercise program and watch your diet—and stick with both. Most obviously, you will start to lose weight and reshape your body.

Also, you will have more energy. You won't be dragging at the end of the day. You will appear more youthful. (Important disclaimer for those of you who might be lawsuit happy: Don't start an exercise program without consulting your physician.) I'm not going to tell you how to get started on this program. It's personal, and you have to do what works for you. I normally get up very early in the morning and go out jogging before work. A friend of mine, a consultant who works from home, finds his energy level decreases around two every afternoon. So he joined a Y and he goes swimming around that time each day.

I don't know how many of you remember the razor blade commercial that went: "To look sharp and to feel sharp, too. . . ." It went on to talk about "the razor that was meant for you." But for me as an adult it was always the first part that mattered. When I looked good, I felt good, and when I felt good, I was always a far more productive salesperson.

In that regard, purchase new business apparel. Your older suits don't fit as well. Treat yourself. Who deserves it more than you? You will feel better for it, and I'm confident that the results in terms of increased sales will make it all worthwhile—even if you use an expensive tailor.

SHAKING THINGS UP MENTALLY

Recuperate by refocusing. I'm going to be talking a lot about refocusing in upcoming chapters: refocusing on what you did well when you were a younger salesperson, refocusing on the basics of selling. The refocusing I refer to now is to refocus on yourself. Take a little "me time."

If you are a sales professional in his or her mid-forties or older, selling almost certainly represents the longest cycle in your life. Unless you came to the profession later on, you've been selling longer than you went to school and longer than you've been married.

If you've been good at it (and once again my assumption because you're reading this book is that the answer is yes), you've spent most of that time pleasing other people. You worked hard to find good deals for your prospects and clients. You worked hard to please your boss; and while there was certainly a substantial amount of ego gratification involved, you worked hard to provide the best things for your family.

And in that time, you've pretty much seen it all. I'm reminded of a scene in a great cop show, *Hill Street Blues*. A criminal turned to a cop who was about to interrogate him and said, "You can't do anything to me that hasn't been done before."

Not that I intend to compare you to a crook, but you've been through the wars. Whether the wars meant international coach travel by plane or thousands of miles in a Ford Taurus, the fact remains you've pretty much seen it all and probably carry your share of scars.

The interesting thing is that no one understands this except you and me. You can tell people about it, but there's really no way for them to relate unless they've put their backsides on those airplane and auto seats, and prepared the presentations and suffered through the rejections. From the outside looking in, a sales career can look glamorous. Who doesn't want to build up that cache of frequent flyer miles? Who wouldn't like a company car? The bonuses? That's easy to see. Less visible is the toll that it takes.

So it's really up to you to fix yourself, to refocus your life at least for the short-term on something other than quotas. You've proven yourself over the years. You don't need to be the number one salesperson every single day. You can be, and you can continue to achieve. But you have nothing left to prove.

Just the other day I spoke to a saleswoman who said she loves selling until the second week of December. That's when she starts developing a terrible case of anxiety about the upcoming year. She's about to start a new year with zero sales in the quota bank. And even though she is one of her company's top salespeople and always exceeds her quota, she gets the willies.

I told her the same thing I'm telling you: Get over yourself and learn to relax. You know that barring something unforeseen you can expect to book X amount of business. You also know that if you put in a minimal effort prospecting for new clients, you'll get X + Y in business. That's what being older can get you: the knowledge that experience brings. So there is no reason for anxiety.

I'm not suggesting that you stop selling or even slow down. But what I think you should do is find a place where you can be content. I'm not going Zen on you, but you have earned the right to spend fifteen, twenty minutes, or even a half-hour each day away from the hullabaloo that is your desk or cubicle. It should be a place where you are not bombarded by phone calls and Emails and bosses. Use that time to think. About whatever you want. Except work. This is a time when you should be able to relax and allow your imagination to run free. Think about what you're going to do with the proceeds when you win the Biggest Mega Lottery in the nation's history. Think about where you'll take your husband or wife to dinner that night. But whatever you do, use that time to refresh yourself.

Two other points that may help you refocus:

1. Reorganize your desk. I know that sounds pretty silly, but I've found that when I clean out the load of useless, eh . . . stuff—yes, that's it, stuff—and face a clean desk, it's sort of like a fresh start, a renewal. It also is an opportunity to simplify your life a little. It works for me every time (I do it once a year), and students to whom I've recommended this rave about it.

2. Treat yourself like a client. I suggest that you have lunch every day at a restaurant with white tablecloths—whether you're with a client or not. Most of us rush through breakfast and on most days come home to pizza or leftovers. We never spend time enjoying a meal. Yet that single act can make you feel comfortable and relaxed.

13

KNOW YOUR WORTH

When I first got serious about my sales career I thought I was the hottest thing going. I was pretty successful, and when I semi-switched my career from selling to teaching selling, I thought I knew it all. How wonderful was I to share my wisdom with the great, unwashed masses?

But something interesting and in many ways wonderful happened along the way from there to here: I learned how much I didn't know. It didn't happen always, but once every six or seven classes, a student would ask a question that forced me to rethink a basic tenet of my sales philosophy.

It's been over three decades since I founded my sales training business. And I don't get quite as many breakthrough ideas as I did earlier in my career. But still, every once in a while, a student asks a question that stumps me and forces me to rethink a precept I'd held dearly.

But that is what maturity and experience is all about. You've spent years making deposits in your wisdom bank. Now there's no reason you can't flaunt it. When it comes to sales, you really didn't get older, you got better—and, more important, smarter.

That is not to say that everyone with a lot of experience is a sales genius. But it does mean that you have the potential to be a genius, because you've probably mastered the three main elements of sales: prospecting, presentation, and product knowledge.

Prospecting and presentation skills are something you learn early on in your career. But product knowledge is something that comes only with experience. No one knows your products as well as you do. And by that I don't mean just its technical specifications. I mean everything.

You've learned its strengths and its weaknesses. You've learned how to overcome specific objections. More important, you know the product's malleability. That is, you know how to mold it and shape it so that you can find a way to make it meet a customer's needs.

But don't expect to get any special recognition for this expertise. If you're expecting awards, you'll be sorely disappointed. Any recognition has to come from within. You have to be your own champion. I'm going to be discussing this further later in the book, but there is a thought on this subject I want to leave you with:

If you're not promoting yourself and you don't understand the value of self-promotion at this point in your career you are doing an injustice to yourself.

Of course, experience brings other benefits, too. Your extended storehouse of knowledge enables you to do everything else well. Unlike a younger salesperson who rattles through a call, you have the ability to have a conversation. Unlike a younger sales rep, who is thrown for a loop when a prospect has a problem or objection, you've heard it all and seen it all, and you know how to respond.

And unlike the younger sales rep, you don't need a manager to hold your hand. You know what to do and when to do it. You hold magic keys, and at times you have to ask yourself if your company values that. If not, you clearly haven't been doing a good job when it comes to self-promotion. You have a major competitive edge over some newcomer, and the boss ought to know about it.

KNOW YOUR WORTH

But none of this works if you don't understand your value to the company. In one of my classes, I ran into a salesman who was about forty-five years old at the time. Let's call him Don. Don had been with the same company his entire professional career and was always among the top three salesmen in a large company. Let me be clear: He wasn't in the top three in his region. He was in the top three in the entire U.S. operation of a large international corporation. The problem is that he worked for a real SOB. His boss took all the credit for any of Don's innovations.

And Don let him. He'd been brought up in a family that had what I call a Depression mentality. I wasn't privy to the entire story, but from what I gather, Don's grandfather lost his job during the Depression and was out of work for a long time. That weighed heavily on Don's dad, who instilled in Don a don't-rock-the-boat mentality at work. He taught Don that all bosses are bastards, and that you have to put up with crap because the job is what's important.

I think that that's an extreme case. Most people who consistently finish as the top salesperson at a company pick up a modicum of confidence along the way. But not Don. When I pointed out the inconsistency of his professional life outlook, Don didn't see it. What he was doing seemed perfectly natural to him. I could never convince him that he was more valuable to the company than the company was to him.

But I'm sure you see that in Don's case. And even if you're not among the top salespeople in your company now, your experience and wisdom is important, and the company will likely lose more than it gains if you leave. If you do not believe that, you won't convince anyone else of it.

Bullies pick on the weakest. It's the same with rotten bosses.

14

THE BIG IDEA

I'm asked to speak about sales once or twice a month. The groups vary in size—from several dozen to several hundred. The one thing they pretty much share in common is that they've all been there and done that.

What I mean is that going in, to them I'm just another sales trainer. Actually, my mission is to speak to them on a topic selected by the people paying my exorbitant fee, not to do training. But I understand why they have that been-there, done-that feeling. They've probably seen dozens of people like me over the course of their careers. In fact, one thing I always ask is: How many of you have ever attended a sales training session? Pretty much everybody raises their hands.

Usually, there is no one in the audience who has not gone through this experience before. I tell them that's why I'm a commodity. In their eyes, I'm interchangeable with dozens of other sales trainers they've experienced. I don't say that to put myself down. We probably look identical to the people we train. We're almost like whooping cranes. Remember that old saying: If you've seen a dozen whooping cranes you've seen them all. For most people, if you've seen one sales trainer, you've seen them all.

Of course I exaggerate. There certainly are differences between us, between good and not-so-good sales trainers. And by that of course I mean between me and everyone else. And that difference is the Big Idea.

I don't have a generic speech. I do a lot of research when I'm asked to give a talk. Who will I address? What kinds of positions do they hold in their companies? Are they managers or salespeople? What products do they sell?

Of course, it would be easier and less time-consuming for me to give a generic speech. After all, I got the job already. But I'm not worried about just this job, but about my next one and the one after that. I'm worried about my reputation. So every time I give a speech I try to come up with at least one Big Idea—a concept, a thought so thoroughly new, so completely appropriate to my audience that I immediately rise in their esteem. I am no longer a commodity. I am special.

WHAT SEPARATES YOU FROM THE PACK?

With all due respect, can we apply the same standards to you as a salesperson? My most recent speech was to an audience of medical supply salespeople. They were all veterans in the field. And while they hadn't all worked for their present employer throughout their careers, most had spent their entire professional lives in the same field. They'd spent twenty, thirty, and more years selling essentially the same products to the same doctors, nurses, and medical supply houses.

I challenged them to tell me something that separated one of them from the rest of the pack. And no one could. To be fair, perhaps no one wanted to reveal his Big Idea to a room full of "competitors"—even if they all worked for the same company.

I challenge you now. Can you come up with just one example of a Big Idea that you've offered one of your clients? Or are you still mired in a kind of I'm-just-worried-about-this-sale mediocrity that fails to separate you (and, by extension, your product) from your competitors?

Before you reject this notion, consider what you've been saying to your customers for the last, say, thirty years. No matter what you sell, all I ask is that you look at your career objectively. When you started, your youth and enthusiasm counted a lot. It allowed you to sell without having to delve very deeply into the intricacies of your product. In some cases, buyers were willing to overlook slipups because they recognized that you were new to the business, new to sales, and the "cute kid."

But that could only go so far. At some point, you were held accountable for your sales actions. You could no longer use your kiddy status and exuberance and brawn to win sales. You had to rely on your brains. And that is even more important for you now.

Because of your years of experience in the industry, it's likely that your customers will rely on you for their expertise. Frankly, don't you want your prospects to do the same? Whenever anyone needs the Big Idea, you want them to turn to you. Whenever anyone has a problem you want them to turn to you. Whenever anyone needs a solution you want them to turn to you.

If you're not already doing so, it's important that you think about your clients in a different way and understand the way they use your product. Clearly I don't mean a superficial knowledge, that they attach part "A" of your widget to part "B" of their product. You really should understand the nuances of the clients' processes, from manufacturing to marketing. That's the only way you'll come up with credible, intelligent, masterful suggestions that will add value to the product: in essence, the Big Idea.

Dig deeply beyond the superficial

The sad truth of the matter is that most people only sell superficially. Part of the reason for that is that they don't have the experience necessary to offer ideas that carry weight. But—and I know I'm repeating myself— that's exactly the point of this book. Instead of getting depressed about getting older in the business, you should be reveling in it. You might very well be able to show your clients uses for their products that they'd never thought of.

Imagine going to someone's office or the shop floor and saying you have an idea for them. The words "idea" and "imagine" are the most powerful words you can use, a platform allowing you to sell deeper into a customer. Imagine this idea working for you.

Here's an example: One of my favorite salespersons sold ball bearings. I love ball bearings. They're so simple and at the same time so complicated.

He was running into a lot of trouble because of competition from overseas. Imports were good enough and a lot cheaper. So he carefully examined the way the ball bearings were being used, and came back with a recommendation that revolutionized the company and saved the account.

What he suggested was simple. His company would help assemble the product. He'd send raw product already containing ball bearings to the client for final assembly. And because of the two companies' proximity, he was able to promise just-in-time delivery. So everyone came out ahead:

The salesman's company came out ahead, because it got back an account it had lost and now had an opening into a new business. The client company came out ahead, because it saved money by having some assembly done elsewhere and because it no longer needed to stockpile ball bearings. And of course the salesman came out ahead, because his Big Idea earned him a lot of money and a great reputation.

That's creative thinking. That's the Big Idea.

Consider the arborist who had a lot of dead time in the winter. He came up with a plan for surveying trees to prepare for spring pruning and plantings. Not only did he pick up additional business, but, because of his relationship with the client, also landed the snow plowing account.

Consider the carpenter who came to my vacation home to build a simple cabinet, looked around, and made suggestions about wooden floors and new shelves. I will not tell you how big a deal he walked away with. But that was another Big Idea.

No insult to landscapers or carpenters, but if they can come up with Big Sales Ideas, don't you think you can? After all, that's your business. You have the same capacity. You might argue it takes time to build up that kind of knowledge and relationship. Well, what have you been doing all these years?

A friend of mine sent me a proverb I hung on my office wall:

"The best time to plant a tree was twenty years ago. The second best time is today."

GROWING OLDER

GARY DAVID GOLDBERG

*Gary David Goldberg is an Emmy Award–winning writer
and producer. He created the television series* Family Ties
and cocreated Spin City. *A few years ago he quit Hollywood
and now lives on a farm in Vermont.*

I'm actually enjoying getting older, I think. Except for my knees, which are purely decorative at this point, most other moving parts are holding up nicely. And, there's a perspective creeping in that is very calming and satisfying. It certainly helps that my wife Diana is well and our kids are well and happy.

I'm never bored in Vermont. We joke that we don't really do anything but we can't find the time to do it. The five big dogs are a very large and dominating part of our life there. And, our day revolves around them. We walk about eight to ten miles a day through our woods—never a need to be on a leash for us or the dogs. We read a lot. Take nice naps. Drink some wine. It's really satisfying in a very deep way. I'm actually not truly comfortable anymore being away from the farm for any length of time. Turns out I'm bucolic. Who knew?

As time went on [in Hollywood] there seemed to be way too many people at the networks who felt that they had an obligation and a right to discuss your work. And, who seemed to not understand the process of doing a weekly show at all. And, that would get frustrating. Mostly, it just sucked up time and energy. It culminated for me with young a woman who after we had made a casting choice said to me "That's not what I had in my head." And, I replied, "Well, here's the interesting thing. It's not in your head it's in my head. Because if it was in your head you'd be me. And, you'd be good."

And, after that I felt like a mean old guy because even though I was right it wasn't a fair fight. And, as the executives got younger the problem for me was that they weren't equal fighting partners. Many of them had grown up on *Family Ties*. And, given the extreme difference in our age it seemed hard for me to actually get mad, because it was like getting mad at one of your kids and equally unsatisfying. Overall, I loved working with much younger people. And, of course the very young writers on *Spin City*. Loved the energy and enthusiasm and careless obsession they brought with them. Just loved it. Loved being from another world and seeing our worlds collide.

What changed was my approach to the work as I felt the absolute overwhelming, obsessive compulsion to dominate and control events start to slip away—which I believe is a good thing.

[Finally,] I believe Alex Keaton is doing pro bono legal work for the Children's Defense Fund. Mike Fox thinks he's just now getting out of jail.

The Career Salesperson

PART

REENERGIZING YOURSELF

15

LIVING OFF THE BOOK

Allow me to recap a couple of points I made earlier in this book (in some cases, several times): It is a scientific fact that every human in the known universe gets the middle-aged blahs. When I started writing the book, I based this axiom mostly on empirical data. That is, pretty much every middle-aged person I knew had it, so it had to be true.

But, suddenly, eureka! Science confirmed my theory. It's perfectly normal. Everyone gets the middle-aged blahs. Although this next part may change by the time you read this, sadly science has not yet confirmed the rest of that theory. I stress the word *yet*. Part two of my theory is that salespeople are more likely to be affected by these blahs than most people. It's obvious, at least to me.

Selling is a pressure-filled job. And it's a constant pressure. No disrespect intended, but it's not like we're accountants. From January to April 15 accountants are under a lot of pressure. But for most of the rest of the year . . . well, not so much.

Moreover, ours is a public contact job. So we have to be on all the time. Bad days affect our bottom line. If we're sad or angry, we still have to put on a happy face.

Add to that the problems of dealing with disrespectful kids—babies really—as prospects, customers, even bosses, and it's easy to see why the world's scientists will soon gather at my feet for even more tidbits of wisdom.

Having said all that, I understand why a salesperson might want to coast, to live off his book. Who deserves it more? I know that I was tempted to do it; I've already admitted that. Maybe what I went through will sound familiar to you. Without getting too specific, I was at that age when the blahs begin to threaten. My business had thrived, but professionally I was at a particularly bad point.

A company that represented a significant share of my business was purchased by an even larger corporation that seemed to have absolutely zero interest in training. At about the same time, a prospect I'd spent an awful lot on—emotionally, intellectually, time-wise and of course financially—decided against using me.

EASING UP ISN'T THE ANSWER

While I hit a rough patch professionally, my personal life was going great guns. My two daughters were both out of college—and out of the house. I had a really good book of business. And while I was still a relatively young man, I felt I was at a place in time where it was okay for me to cut back. If I closed my expensive New York City office and worked out of my home, we'd be okay.

Several things happened at about the same time that made me change my mind. The first was graduate school. How could I not help out my daughters? Second, my wife made it clear that the only thing she'd like more than me working at home was the plague.

In addition to expressing distaste (to put it mildly) at spending both day and night in my company, she said something I thought particularly wise. She asked me, "What would you tell one of your students under the same circumstances? Would you suggest that she cut back? Or would you find a way to help her work through it, so that she didn't unnecessarily hurt what had been a good career?" I knew the answer, of course. However, the truth is I find it a lot easier to give advice than take it.

Then I met a close friend for our monthly luncheon. We met when I was a young, single guy and he was just starting in the life insurance business. It was a second career for him, but one where he quickly found his niche. He sold me a policy. And when I got married he sold me a bigger one. And when I had kids . . . well, you get the picture. He soon had a very profitable book of business. In addition to my insurance agent, he became a close friend and sounding board. We met at least once a month. When I was debating whether or not I could live off my book, it was natural for me to consult him.

Several years earlier, he told me, he'd taken the step I was contemplating. He decided to live off his substantial book. The revenue that generated afforded him a very comfortable lifestyle. What he hadn't counted on was how quickly his book shrank. Many of the people to whom he'd sold life policies were dying. His book was getting smaller faster than he'd anticipated. In essence, what happened to me with the sizable account that died happened to him with a lot of small accounts.

Also, while he was still technically employed selling insurance, he rarely prospected for new clients. And he found he missed the action. But more than that, he missed the money. The good news is this. Getting back to the action was easier than he expected—which is bringing us dangerously close to the moral of this tale.

What happened was that he went back to his book clients. Because they dealt with him, because he'd proven his wisdom over the years, he found them willing—even eager—to give him bigger orders. These people he'd taken for granted over the last few years hadn't forgotten him—even if he'd momentarily forgotten them. They were also happy to recommend him to their friends, and soon his business started to grow.

He also looked at his customer base and reinvented himself. While he was still getting some younger customers buying their first insurance policy—often the children of those he sold to years ago—he reinvented himself as an expert in estate planning. This allowed him to go after an entirely new market.

Reinvention and selling forever are topics we'll cover, but I do want to conclude for now by saying that relying on your book is almost always a bad idea. It's more than just the fact that your book may not last as long as you do. It's also that doing that makes you lazy. Not only do you stop

16

GET OVER YOURSELF

Earlier I mentioned a sales executive I met en route to a Florida vacation. There's more to that story. As noted, he was the vice president of sales for an international printing company.

Experienced salesman that I am, I managed to segue the conversation from his sales problems to my sales solutions. He agreed with everything I had to say. He said, yes, that's exactly the kind of program he needed. He was home from an extended business trip so he didn't have any spare business cards. I wrote down his e-mail address on a piece of paper and said I'd contact him when I got back to my office.

I had no reason to believe that he wasn't sincere. We were roughly the same age, and although we didn't know each other or have anyone in common, we grew up not that far from each other. It wasn't a done deal, but I was feeling pretty good. I'd scored a client on vacation. How good am I?

Well, you know the rest of this story, don't you? I sent him an e-mail. No response. Well, I rationalized, maybe he didn't get it. Things get screwed up. So I sent him another. No response. What are the odds that two consecutive e-mails might get lost in the ether?

Why take a chance? I looked the company up on the web and called, leaving him a message. Again I received no response. By now I'm getting a little steamed. I mention this incident to a friend of mind who is much nicer and far more forgiving than I am. He says, "The guy works for an international company. He's on the road a lot. Be patient. Give him another shot."

So I called him again, and he picked up the phone. It took him a second, but he remembered me. Yes, of course, he was interested. But he was on his way out to a meeting. He'd call me either later that afternoon or the next day. That was four weeks ago.

YOU CAN'T TAKE IT PERSONALLY

This particular episode got the better of me. You win some, and you lose some. I know people prefer to avoid you rather than give you bad news. I understand that. But this guy had nothing vested in me, and I had nothing vested in him. All he had to do is say, "I checked, and I really don't have a budget this year." He's a salesman, for goodness sakes. Is this the way he'd want to be treated?

It really annoyed me, and I dwelled on it much longer than I should have. It got the better of me. Remember the old sawhorse about the economy: If two million people are unemployed in the U.S., the country is in a recession. If you're unemployed, the nation is in a depression.

It's perfectly natural to take things to heart. I do. I know when I work hard to land an account, when I've done my homework, when I make a presentation that is logical, persuasive, when I show a prospect how my classes can help his sales force improve its sales, and I still get turned down, how can I not take it personally? That buyer had to be stupid not to take what I offered.

These experiences tend to build on one another, like compound interest. The bad news is that they can't help but contribute to that general malaise that infects us at midlife. Often it's hard to keep from carrying that malaise with you and spreading the infection. By that, I mean that walking in to my next appointment still upset about the last turndown could affect this one. It's like when a smoker walks into a room and the odor of cigarettes follows him. For me after one of those I shoulda-had-that-contract defeats, the negativity I brought with me to my next few appointments probably hung heavily in the air. And if I didn't get that deal, my negativity grew even more.

THE FAT LADY SANG; MOVE ON

Slumps are part of the game. And typically ballplayers and salespeople press harder instead of relaxing and going with the flow. Then everything starts to fall apart—and like Humpty Dumpty, it gets harder to put back together again.

But there is good news. All those years that contributed to midlife crises also gave you the experience to get over some of them. If you are forty to fifty years old and have never run into a slump, you are likely the *Book of Records* salesperson that the people at Guinness have been looking for.

The rest of us know that this, too, shall pass. It doesn't make it any easier, or, given our temperaments, any less likely that we won't dwell on and worry about it. But you have to get over yourself. Here are some suggestions that have worked for me and many of my students to triumph over these self-imposed obstacles.

GET A GRIP

Come to grip with the fact that there's very little you can do about obstacles except worry—and that's counterproductive. Worrying about whether or not you sign a deal after you've done all you can to make it happen is as useless as my telling you not to worry. But I have to try.

LAUGH AT YOURSELF

I've long felt (and written) that no one wakes up in the morning intending to be stupid. But sometimes we do stupid things. Sometimes they are so stupid, they're funny.

Here's an example of how stupid I can be. I was networking at a convention and met Bill, the vice president of sales for a company I'd frankly never heard of. I exchanged conversation and business cards with him, promising to get in touch when I returned to my office. Perhaps half an hour later I ran into Denise, who worked for a firm that competed with Bill's on some product lines. We also spoke and exchanged cards. But it was Bill who'd expressed the most interest in discussing my courses.

When I returned to New York I could not find Bill's card. I searched my wallet, I searched my little business card holder, but I couldn't find it. I wasn't sure of his name or the company he worked for, and frankly cursed my carelessness.

The good news was I still had Denise's card. So I dropped her a line, reminded her of our meeting, and said I'd follow up with a phone call to set up an appointment. When I called she laughed and picked up the phone. "So there really is a Stephan Schiffman," she said. I didn't understand what she meant.

"At first I thought you were Bill X trying to spy on me."

I still didn't understand. But when we sorted things out I had to laugh, too. Apparently, when I reached into my card holder to give her my card, I inadvertently gave her Bill's card I'd collected just minutes earlier. Yes, she made the appointment, and yes, I sold her a program. She also returned Bill's card to me, and yes, I called him and explained why it took me so long to get in touch. We also had a good laugh about what happened, and although it took a while, he eventually signed with me, too.

My point is that what I thought was a really stupid mistake on my part—losing Bill's card—turned out to be beneficial. We all got a kick out of my mistake, and I probably wound up with more business than I would have if I hadn't screwed up.

I've made silly mistakes since then, but somehow they don't bother me as much as they used to. All I have to do is think of the business card fiasco. And I start to smile. Also, it's a great anecdote I've told more than once to loosen things up after I've just met someone. We exchange cards, and I make a great show of checking that my name is on the one I give him.

Spend time thinking about the good things in your life.

I know it sounds a lot like psychobabble, but it works. If you have a good family life, think about hearth and home, your kids and your grandchildren, when things get tough. A friend of mine, also a consultant, has two granddaughters. He's always been wrapped up in his work, worrying about where his next client is coming from and feels guilty about not having spent enough time with his kids. But he claims he's given up worrying. Whenever he gets down, he thinks about his granddaughters, and he says, "I can't help but smile. I feel like my face glows." It works.

I know someone else who regularly volunteers at a soup kitchen. "Do that," he tells me, "and your troubles will seem trivial."

Laughter really is the best medicine

I don't know how many of you read *Reader's Digest*, but the magazine has a regular column with that title. Believe it or not, it works. Norman Cousins, a famous magazine editor, was extremely ill and confined to his bed. He procured old Laurel & Hardy and Abbott & Costello movies and literally laughed himself well. Read his *Anatomy of an Illness*, which chronicles his miraculous recovery. When I get down, I quickly make my way to a comedy club. It's amazing what a young comic can do for my spirits. If that is inconvenient I rerun *Beetlejuice,* my favorite comedy of all time. You will love it, assuming your sense of humor is slightly off kilter as mine is.

Read biographies of people of achievement

Invariably, these books are inspirational. More to the point, many of these leaders and achievers have done something in their lives—some rule they live by, some philosophy they've adopted—that you can use in your own life. As a corollary to that, when I drive to work or an appointment, I listen to the traffic report and immediately shut the radio. The news is filled with negativity, and I don't need that when I'm on my way to meet a client. Instead I pop in one of those you-can-do-it, rousing, moving CDs that will encourage me and spur me on.

THINK

A few years ago I was sitting in my comfort chair at home, just thinking. My youngest daughter came in and asked me, "What's the matter?"

I said, "Nothing. I'm just thinking."

Then my oldest daughter came and said, "Why are you upset?"

I said, "Nothing's wrong. I'm just thinking."

Then my wife came in and said, "I hear you're upset."

Part of the problem with life is that people won't let you think. Either the phone is ringing or the boss wants to speak to you or you're racing out to an appointment. You have to find a time and place where you can think. You need some alone time. That will help put a proper perspective on whatever it is that's bothering you.

The Career Salesperson

17

Tomorrow Always Comes (The Tough Love Chapter)

Somewhere in the past, in the midst of a deep philosophical discussion, someone said to me, "Tomorrow always comes." I honestly do not remember who said it or in what context it was said. But I do remember being struck by the thought. In fact, the next day I had the saying printed up, mounted and framed, and put it in a prominent place in my office.

I guess it can mean different things to different people, depending in large measure on where you are in your life and career. But to me it is another commandment to get over yourself. I chose the word "commandment" carefully. Because unless another Old Testament prophet like Joshua can get God to stop the sun in the sky, tomorrow will come.

Tomorrow won't care about what happened today. It won't care that you're sulking. Or that you're feeling badly. Or that your new boss doesn't like you. Tomorrow always comes.

You don't have to be a mature salesperson to sulk or feel badly or fret about the future. But the older you are, the more difficult it is to come to grips with what's happened to you. If you are twenty-four or twenty-five years old and you lose a client or a sure-thing sale turns out not to be so sure, well there is tomorrow. There still is that rainbow, and you can ride it until the end where you get the pot of gold. Your dreams are as fresh as they ever were.

But let's say you're forty-five, and suddenly you see young kids in positions of authority. You realize the possibility that you will never live your dream. That whatever the possibilities you thought you had when you were in your twenties will probably never happen. But, like the hide and seek game you played as kids, ready or not, here comes tomorrow.

That sounds far harsher than I intend it to. There is absolutely nothing wrong with a career in sales. It's an opportunity to make an awful lot of money and enjoy a certain amount of freedom. But remember, please, something I said earlier on in this book. Most of us didn't set out to be salespeople. I believe most of us wanted to go elsewhere in the corporate hierarchy and saw sales or sales experience as a way to get there. Then stuff happened. Maybe the money was so good so quickly it became difficult to get out. Maybe we actually enjoyed sales. But, for whatever reason, this is where we are, in a place we didn't intend to be when we first thought about where we were going.

GET ON THE REALITY RIDE

But I've come to think of it as positive—or at least potentially positive. This is the period where we separate from the boys from the men, the girlish dreams from the womanly reality.

The reality is that not everyone gets to play in the Major Leagues. Some people who don't make it become misanthropes. Others are smarter and make other careers for themselves, as scouts or managers, or they coach high school and college teams. Or they become salespeople. Boys and girls believe that every cloud has a silver lining. Adults understand that every silver lining has a cloud.

The difference between us and them is that we've been through the wars. Over a lifetime in sales, this has become familiar terrain for us. Been there, done that. And we may not realize it, but (with apologies to Jerry Seinfeld) we are masters of our domain. I didn't understand that at first. But I came to realize that I controlled my own destiny.

The main thing you have to do is establish a new vision for yourself. Why should you be tied to a dream you had twenty or thirty years ago?

The Career Salesperson

When you were a kid you wanted to be a cop or fireman; you got over that, didn't you?

You're not the kid fresh out of college determined to become CEO of the world's largest corporation. So let's take a look at your life now. There are a lot of "yous" out there, so I'm going to draw a composite. The chances are you have to continue working, either because you want to or you have to (probably the latter). You may still have children who need to be educated or pension plans that need to be fattened.

It doesn't make a difference. The point is that you can work smarter now than you have in the past. When you prospect, you know every trick to get through to a potential customer, every reason he or she has to say "no," and every way to turn him or her around.

In short, you know how to work smart. You may not have been doing that lately, but you know how. It's just a question of getting back into the habit of doing things you may have overlooked.

BRING IT ON!

But taking control of your life is more than just reinventing yourself at work. That alone won't help. You have to reexamine your dreams. I would have written this even if I were not made aware of the survey results: you are entering the best, most enjoyable years of your life. You will never be as productive at work as you can be now. But also things will likely get better for you outside of work as well.

At some point soon, the financial pressures will decrease substantially. You'll become an empty nester, responsible only for yourself and significant other. The mortgage is paid off. So I ask you again: Tomorrow always comes, what are you going to do?

Forget about being CEO of the world's largest company. Become CEO of your life. What is it that you always wanted to do? Take piano lessons? Learn how to paint? Buy a sail boat? Whether you realize it or not, these are the best years of your life. You can finally have it all. So when tomorrow comes, you'll be ready to say, "Bring it on!"

GROWING OLDER
LARRY GELBART

Larry Gelbart is an award-winning screen and television writer, creator of the television series M*A*S*H.

I seem to have more ideas than ever. Perhaps they come in such abundance because I know down deep that I don't have the nearly enough time required to see all of them through to completion. There's still fire in the belly (and decidedly more belly than that), but, again, time serves as a great fire extinguisher.

PART V

USING YOUR WISDOM

18

SELLING IN THE TWENTY-FIRST CENTURY

Selling has undergone a tremendous metamorphosis over the last three or four decades. When I first got into the business, salesmen—we were all men, back then—relied on gimmicks and guile as much as we relied on our brains.

A couple of examples should suffice. I knew a guy who used to mail a shoe to a potential client with a note saying this was his way of getting a foot in the door.

Another guy photocopied his face so the prospect would recognize him. While that certainly was far better than other bodily parts commonly Xeroxed, it still falls far short of being an intelligent way to catch a prospect's attention. A smart client doesn't care what you look like. He or she cares about what you can deliver.

The world's economy has become far too competitive to allow anyone to make decisions based on gimmicks. You have to use your smarts—and I'm confident that most of you know that.

That's why this should be the shortest chapter in the book. Let me explain.

THREE KINDS OF SALESPEOPLE

Over the course of my career, I've trained more than half a million sales-people, and I've walked away from them with a keener understanding of the sales process and the people who are in it. One of the most important things I've learned is that while there are essentially two kinds of sales-people—hunters and farmers—they fall into three categories.

There are those for whom sales comes easily, the way that Michael Jordan used to score. They were born to it.

There are those who are good at sales, but mostly because they work hard at it. What comes naturally to those who are gifted in sales requires a lot of practice from these people. Carrying the basketball analogy one step further, I'm thinking of Chris Mullins, the St. John's University/NBA great who wasn't as athletically gifted as Jordan, so became a gym rat instead, spending hours alone shooting baskets.

The final category is about "sales" people—and I purposely use quotes—who are merely order takers. These guys don't make it to the pros and probably don't even play backyard games anymore, because it's too much effort. These are people essentially trapped in the wrong profession and just trying to get by.

My assumption in writing this book is that the people who read it fall into the first two categories. Even the most gifted salespeople, even the greatest and most successful workaholics get older. No one is exempt from this. But I have the feeling that all of you sold the new way; perhaps many of you still do—if not exactly with the same fervor you once did. So the good news is that this isn't a chapter about how to sell. It's a chapter on using your accumulated wisdom to making selling easier.

SELLING SMART

Selling smart manifests itself in several ways. But the single most impor-tant thing to come to grips with is that selling smart is less a function of a particular technique or techniques, but confidence. By that, I mean no matter how depressed you are, it is incumbent upon you to remember that negativity doesn't sell. You might lose a dozen sales in a row. Your new boss may consider you a relic. Your biggest account may suddenly be controlled by a teenager. But you have memory, memory that can (if you let it) restore your spirit. And you have wisdom garnered by traveling down these same roads so many times before. And that alone should break you out of your funk.

CARRY YOUR WISDOM WELL

Here's what you know that the young'uns don't (or at least don't know as well):

You know more about your product than anyone. You know the obvious, but you also know its malleability—that is the way it can be changed ever so slightly from its traditional use to fit the needs of a customer.

You understand the meaning of sales team. You understand that you have to think like the prospect, not like a salesperson. It isn't you vs. them. It's we're all in this together. So you've built up systems to get the prospect involved in the sales, to get him or her on your team.

Your experience has taught you to ask the right questions to elicit the information you need. Your job, you know, is not to make the sale, but to help the prospect do whatever he or she is doing better and/or less expensively.

You pick up clues better and analyze faster than a rookie. In fact, if you're selling to someone much younger than you are, he or she might respect you for your expertise substantially more than a relative newcomer to sales who has more limited knowledge of product and technique. Let me give you a personal example. At sixty-two I feel I have a distinct advantage over ninety percent of the senior vice presidents of sales I typically sell to. This is true not only because I'm older, but because I've worked with more companies than they're likely to in a lifetime. The average salesperson will have ... what? Three or four jobs in their adult lives? I've worked with more than 900 companies. And when I say worked with, I mean delved into the way they operate their sales organizations and relate to customers. I have more experience with more sales forces than they do.

I recently gave a speech on prospecting techniques to the sales force of a large company. Ironically, just today when I'm hard at work on this chapter, I received an e-mail from the person who hired me to give the speech. He asked for my advice on how he can reinforce the lessons I spoke about, how he could follow up to make the training more effective. I, of course, suggested that some of the very training courses I offered might fit the bill. It is too early to tell if he'll follow my advice, but the point I want to make in this case isn't about a sale.

Here is a case where one of my customers, a sales manager much younger than I am, came to me looking for expertise. My guess is that you've been on hundreds, probably thousands, of sales calls over the course of your career. In your industry, you probably have experience comparable to mine.

Think about what that means. Think about how much money you've brought in for the companies you've worked for and how much you helped the companies that you've sold to. Think about what that means. Think about how far you've traveled over the last twenty or thirty years. By that I don't mean just the road miles you've traveled, but the maturity miles.

Seriously, can you remember what a crummy salesman you used to be? You do things now you never could have done two or three decades ago. I think you should take pride in what you've accomplished over the years. And that pride combined with confidence and experience will carry you to new heights—no matter how old you are.

19

PROSPECTING

When God wanted to punish Adam and Eve he banished them from the Garden of Eden. When he wanted to punish salespeople, he invented the cold call. I still debate which is worse on the severity scale.

I believe that the more experienced a salesperson becomes, the easier it is to prospect. But the reality is that no matter how experienced you are, the idea of prospecting still strikes fear into your heart.

The chances are that over the years you developed your own techniques for prospecting—and even more and better techniques for avoiding the task. I found the key to cold calling in two basic principles.

IT ISN'T PERSONAL

The first is that it isn't personal. Initially as a young salesman, I was offended when people didn't call me back or refused to see me. I had this great product and it would be a matter of simple courtesy to see me. Back then, I'd feel hurt and a failure. It was my job to make them see me, and I couldn't make it happen.

Frankly, it took a while for me to get over it. (Actually, I'm not *completely* cured; I still have moments of melancholy when I can't get through to a much sought-after prospect.) But for the most part I've come to realize that it isn't personal. It couldn't be me, since the prospect doesn't know me.

There are myriad reasons she doesn't return my calls or make an appointment. But the major reason is inertia. If no one is complaining about the product the company currently uses, why upset the apple cart? Once I came to that realization, prospecting became easier for me. Not simple, mind you. Just easier.

Second, you have to make—force—prospecting to become an ingrained habit. I made myself make a certain number of calls every day for weeks on end—to the point where it became second nature to me. The first thing I did every single day I was in the office was make calls to ten new prospects. By new prospects, I don't mean followup calls (calls to people I've contacted previously don't count). And I refused to leave my desk until I'd made at least ten calls.

It became a habit, and as with pretty much everything you practice regularly, you get better at it. I started to anticipate every possible objection and developed reasoned, thoughtful, and intelligent responses. In relatively short order, I started getting more appointments, making more presentations, and frankly becoming increasingly successful. I had my version of a large book: super-sized international corporations who would use my training programs year after year.

PROSPECTING IS THE KEY TO SUCCESS

Soon I wasn't in the office as much as I used to be. And when I was there, there was a lot of paperwork to do, bills to send out, followups to previous calls. And pretty soon prospecting became a rare event rather than the habit it once was. This chapter is intended to remind you that the ability to prospect is usually the key to a salesperson's success. And even if you're feeling the midlife blues, prospecting is the key to your comeback—even if you never left.

As noted, you probably have developed your own techniques. The key to whatever success you will have prospecting comes from what is a recurring theme of this book: confidence and understanding that if properly harnessed, all your experience and accumulated wisdom can work for you.

For example, one of the first things I tell a cold call prospect I get on the phone is the experience I've had, the books I've written, the companies I've worked with and the staggering numbers of salespeople I've trained over the last three decades. I want the prospect to understand that I'm not someone who calls fishing for leads, but I am an expert, a force to be reckoned with, someone he should not easily dismiss.

Ironically, someone recently used the same tactic on me. I always answer my own phone, and this time it was a salesman. He caught me at a bad time, and I was trying to get him off the phone as politely as I could. He must have sensed that, because he stopped me cold, saying:

"Listen, Steve. I'm fifty-seven years old and I've been working for this company for thirty years. Believe me, I'm probably right when I say you should meet me."

He commanded my attention by saying he'd done this for so many years. By telling me what to do—that is, see him—he made the process painless for me. Look, let's go back to the widget salesperson—or whatever it is you sell. Why not try that?

"I've been doing this for thirty years, and I understand something about widgets. I can make you a widget that will help you manufacture your product better, with less stress. All I want to do is come up and show you what I've done for other companies and give you an idea of what I can do for you."

Of course, it takes a certain kind of personality to be that confident and—dare I say it?—aggressive. Not everyone has that in him or her. A friend of mine is a writer who developed a course to teach business writing to corporate executives about six years ago. He knew nothing about sales or marketing and was having a trouble marketing a course that was different and (I must admit) pretty much better than anything out in the marketplace.

But he got better. He joined a training association and picked up marketing tips. He honed his presentation skills. And business started coming in—a little more each year. But prospecting was still a chore for him. He found it difficult to make the transition from writer to speaker/salesman. Then lightning struck.

Through a mutual friend who worked there, he got the name of the person who headed the training department at one of the world's largest accounting/consulting firms. She passed him off to one of her associates, Michael, who wasn't anxious to see him. Michael wrote him:

"XX recently forwarded me your marketing packet, since I have oversight responsibility for a large segment of (the company's) nontechnical training curriculum. I recently signed a contract with another vendor, under which they will be developing several training modules similar to what you might be able to provide. While there might be an opportunity sometime down the road, that contract precludes me from pursuing any other vendors in this subject matter at present."

After another series of e-mail exchanges, Michael told my friend to check in the following year in the spring. My friend did so, via e-mail and phone. When he got no reply, he tried once more, and Michael picked up the phone. But he still sent out negative vibes. He said no one was complaining about the current writing course, so he wasn't interested in replacing it. My buddy had no reply for that—until seconds after he hung up the phone. Then he drafted the following in a matter of minutes:

Dear Michael,

I am a better writer than I am debater. I always think of what I should have said to the cop after the ticket is written. Sadly, as soon as I hung up with you a few minutes ago a fully formed argument sprang to mind.

1. I guarantee that the course I offer is sufficiently different and better than what you offer now.

2. I offer services other companies do not. For example, I am currently tutoring an executive at a large financial institution. Because she is

extremely busy during the work day, I travel to her office and work with her from 7 to 9 A.M.

3. Having said all that, I heard what you said. I understand that you are pleased with your current supplier. And, I know, too, that my small operation may not be large enough to handle all your needs. (I deliver all courses myself and do not hire facilitators.) However, I am willing to go to the expense and take the chance that I can convince you to at least give me a try.

4. All I ask is twenty-two minutes for what I call my 1010 WINS* presentation (you give me twenty-two minutes and I'll give you the world of business writing), knowing full well that this is a long shot—at best.

5. I know you are busy, but I issue another guarantee. Even if we don't do any business, you will not feel you have wasted your time.

Twenty minutes? Please?

NEVER GIVE UP

He got the appointment, but not the business . . . yet. Here's what he told me.

It went great, but I ran into what you've been preaching about, the inertia factor. No one is complaining; in fact, people seem to like the course they currently use. So, there's no need to stir things up, to take a chance. But I will get some business. I could tell he was impressed. I'll just stay in touch with him, the way I did with the folks at (a large financial institution).

It took a year and a half between the time he first made contact with the executive director of training and when she finally agreed to see him.

---

*1010 WINS is a New York metropolitan area all-news station whose motto is "Give us twenty-two minutes and we'll give you the world."

During that time, he periodically sent her copies of evaluation reports about his course and copies of news stories about the need for writing skills courses in the corporate environment.

About a year and a half after that she called to say there was an executive who needed tutoring—the exec referred to in the note to Michael. She was a vice president, a valued officer of the company, but she lacked strong writing skills. He tutored her early in the morning, and everyone was pleased with the results. Now my buddy teaches six or seven classes there a year—plus tutoring high-level executives.

He figures the same thing will happen with Michael. Are there lessons to learn here? A couple. First of all, prospecting doesn't necessarily end when a cold call says "not interested." It ain't over until the fat lady (or gentleman) sings.

Also, don't be afraid to use all the tools at your disposal, even e-mail.

Finally, something that's overlooked a lot when discussing cold calling. Depending on the season, a lot of us would love to sit in a warm or air-conditioned office making telephone calls to strangers. But for some sales folk, prospecting means going into an office building, carrying your bag, and knocking on doors.

Prospecting in person puts a higher premium on appearance. Of course, I'm not talking only about your physical appearance—although that's obviously important—but rather the manner in which you carry yourself. If you walk into an office with the weight of the world on your shoulders, a defeatist attitude, there's no way you'll accomplish your goals. But if you walk in, head tall and use your experience, saying to the receptionist:

"Hi, I'm Joe Smith and I've been selling widgets for thirty years, and I've never had a chance to sell to your company before. What I'd like to do is find out who I should call or meet with."

It's an approach that works well because it is nonconfrontational, friendly, and generally people like to be helpful. It's possible the receptionist will tell you that he or she isn't allowed to give out that information. But it is also likely that the receptionist will give you a name, a phone number, and/or an e-mail address. Whatever you get—even if it's just a name—is a good start.

20

A QUICK REVIEW

When I first got into the training business, I delivered my classes and seminars and moved on. Everyone seemed happy, but that changed when an HR woman in charge of one of my clients' training decided to monitor and evaluate my class. You cannot imagine how overjoyed I was when I heard that the boss was going to check me out.

Anyway, I ran my class and met with the woman afterward. Surprise, surprise, she loved my program. In fact, she set up an appointment for later in the week to schedule more classes and to discuss what other programs I might do for the company. And then she said the magic word: "*But!*"

"The class is great, but you never tell them what you are doing. Periodically, you have to review what you've done so far, explain what you did and why you did it, and what you intend to do in the next class period."

My first reaction as a new and relatively inexperienced trainer was that this lady didn't have the faintest idea what she was talking about. From where I stood she was old, inexperienced, and out of touch. (Can you see where I'm going with this?)

However, this tottering, elderly, barely able to walk upright without a cane lady (she must have been all of forty) became my biggest customer.

So what could I do? I thought it was stupid. I believed my students were smart enough to figure out what I was doing. I started doing these little mini-reviews. And you know what? Every once in a while I'd (figuratively) see a light bulb go on over a student's head. Someone I'd given up on suddenly got what I was trying to do. Even better students seemed to benefit from these brief reviews.

This brings me to the points I want to make in this chapter:

1. Even older people can be right. I thought I knew it all and resented the HR lady's suggestions. I was a brash kid—and stupid. But she imparted important wisdom to me, and it made me realize how valuable—and right—she actually was.

2. I've kept true to her wisdom in all my books. So if you look up and see a light bulb over your head, you can blame the HR/training lady. Essentially what I wanted to establish this far is:

- Getting older isn't easy, but it's far more complicated when you work in a high-stress field. Sales is one of those fields, because you always have to be on, and there never seems to be an end to the pressure. You make your nut, and you think life will be easy. But come January 1, you're back at ground zero.
- Everyone gets the blahs. It's important to understand that what you are going through is completely normal. More important, if the scientists are right, you won't be singing the blues forever.
- You can't let the midlife thing get to you. You are a better salesperson now than you ever were—and you're going to get better. Keep that in mind.
- You may be at a point in your life where your expenses are down and you feel you can relax, perhaps live off your book. Resist the temptation. First of all, with any degree of luck you'll likely outlive your book. Second, sales isn't something you can do in a half-hearted way. Either you're a salesperson or you're an order taker.

In today's economy, there's very little room on the staff for order takers.

- At some point, you will be working with what I call young'uns—that is a manager or a customer who is significantly younger than you are. If these people are strangers to you, newcomers brought in from outside, they will be unfamiliar with your accomplishments, the revenue you brought in, and the tough sales you made. They are likely to look at you through the jaundiced eyes of youth—the same way I looked at the HR lady. But the point is that you are not a dinosaur. You have two, three, and four decades of accumulated wisdom. And if you show that wisdom, you will be viewed differently.

- If I had to sum it up in one word, I'd say that the key to success at this time in your life is confidence: confidence that the accumulated knowledge you've built up will carry you over any obstacle.

So what's next? These are perilous times for everyone. Companies merge. Companies cut back. There are layoffs. You may not get along with your new boss, and he may not get along with you. What happens then when you're in your forties, fifties, or even sixties without a job? That's the subject of the next few chapters.

GROWING OLDER
ROBERT PARKER

Robert Parker is the author of mystery novels featuring
Spenser, Jesse Stone and Sunny Randall.

Spenser is ageless. I however, not being fictional, am probably not. And as I evolve so does he. We are both active. I box every Monday and Friday with a martial arts trainer. I lift weights every Tuesday and Thursday. (Joan is much more active than I am. Better looking, too). I work every day at my profession and so does he. We are both, happily for us, keeping long-term company with the girl of our dreams. We are both probably less likely to solve things with a punch in the mouth. Nor, probably, does being the wisest ass in the room matter as much to us as it once did. Neither of us thinks we are old. Except that my knees don't work as well as once they did, I feel as I did when I was forty. While age may foreshorten the future, it doesn't seem like much of a handicap otherwise.

PART

FINDING A NEW JOB

21

THE POSITIVE SIDE
TO CORPORATE
REORGANIZATION—REALLY

There is never a good time to lose your job. But as this is being written, it seems the job situation is worse than ever. Laying off people has become endemic, the almost automatic corporate response to every corporate crisis. Global businesses consolidate. How do you justify the merger? Well, there are increased efficiencies because job duplications—people's jobs—are eliminated. So you lay loyal employees off and, in theory at least, profitability is increased.

Have a bad quarter? You don't want your stock price to go down, so you quickly announce layoffs or buyouts or outright dismissals. It's no longer a question of whether this person is doing a good or bad job; we have to get rid of him, end of story. Everyone, everywhere (with the exception of course of the top executive who got the companies into whatever mess it's in the first place) is being canned, laid off, or excessed or outsourced. But that doesn't make it easier.

Of, course the situation is much worse when the person being let go is "mature." The law forbids discrimination because of age, but you're also supposed to slow down when you see the green light change to yellow. Still people speed up—and are often eager to let older employees go and reluctant to hire anyone of a certain age.

It's hard to quantify how prevalent age discrimination is, but the truth is that we all know it exists. It is one thing to be twenty-five years old and looking for a job, and it's quite another to be forty-five years old. Forget about discrimination, and consider the numbers. The job market is like a triangle, with more jobs at the wide base for beginners than at the top for people with two or three decades' experience. Where does that leave you? How do you handle it if you suddenly find yourself out of work? Here's what I tell people:

1. Losing a job does more than strike a financial blow. It hits hard pschologically, as well. In fact, losing a job is one of the most stressful things that can happen to a man; in terms of its effect on your body, it's comparable to losing a spouse. (I haven't seen any studies on this, but I'm sure that it engenders a substantial amount of stress in women, as well.)

2. Science has discovered that stress weakens your body's immune system. When people say they are sick over losing their job, they may not be kidding. One of the first things you have to come to grips with if this happens to you is its potential impact on your health. You can't look for a job if you're sick.

3. A point I've made repeatedly in this book is that if you are reading it you certainly were and probably still are a top salesperson. In other words, the fact that you are now without a job is in all likelihood not your fault. Nevertheless, you are no longer Joe or Jolene, the top salespeople; you are now Joe or Jolene, another unemployment statistic. For most people who have much of their self-esteem tied to their work, this can be a crushing blow.

4. People will react differently to you. Your family and friends will tiptoe around you. You may become paranoid, convinced that everyone is talking about you. The reference I made a few paragraphs above comparing the stress of being fired being to that experienced when you lose a close family member was quite apt. In fact, a funeral atmosphere sets in. People around you are uncomfortable and don't know what to say.

5. It's okay to be angry, especially if you've spent a long time at this company and given it years of loyalty and sweat. But frustration and rationalization will only take you so far.

A NEW BEGINNING

But there's more than bad news here. All's well that ends well. And losing your job is not the end, it's the beginning. Consider this:

A close friend of mine was a really high level executive in the insurance industry. He worked his way up from an entry level position based solely on the strength of his smarts and excellent work habits. He started in the business directly from high school, going to college at nights (he currently has a master's degree) and worked his way up.

At one point he became a partner in one of the world's largest commercial brokerages. When that company was sold to an ever-larger firm, he quickly proved his mettle. But the politics between executives from the surviving firm and those who came over in the purchase made life there insufferable for my friend.

So he took a buyout and went to work as the number two in a large trade association, with the expectation that the number one was going to leave and that he would replace him. The number one (whom most people wanted ousted) managed to save his job. So my friend took another buyout. And he went to work for another large commercial insurance agency located in the World Trade Center. He started right after Labor Day in 2001. It was pure chance that he wasn't in his office when the plane crashed into his building. But differences with the chairman about who was in charge ultimately resulted in his being out of work again.

This was clearly not an issue about money. He made a fortune from his share as a partner when his first company was bought out. He made even more in severance when he left the trade association. And then even more when he left his last job. Simply: too much of his self-worth was vested in his job.

At roughly about the same time, he went through a tough patch in his personal life; however, it was really the problems at work that seemed to unhinge him. He'd call me once, twice, sometimes even three times a day, spilling his guts about the political travails in his last two jobs that bothered him. He is one of the brightest guys I know, so he had a good idea of what was going on. All he needed was some reassurance.

I think he would have pulled through without me, but what he went through is instructive. What he did was reach out to someone whom he trusted. He was honest about the turmoil he was going through, and I gave him the support and encouragement he needed. He didn't regress into a cocoon. And that ultimately became the first step toward his recovery.

He's now a highly paid consultant who works only when he wants to and enjoys life with his second wife and their adopted child. All's well that ends well.

LOSING A JOB CAN BE AN OPPORTUNITY

My second story involves a much younger friend of mine, a writer. He was about thirty years old the first and only time he was fired. It was unexpected and undeserved. The details don't matter, but it bludgeoned him. He was incapacitated for the longest time. He couldn't sleep. He'd just moved into a house and had two young kids and worried that he wouldn't be able to meet his bills. For the first two weeks, all he could manage was to complete a paint-by-numbers picture. No kidding.

What to do? He was collecting unemployment insurance, he had a couple of weeks' severance pay, and he had two weeks' vacation pay. So he knew he was okay for about a month. Then he'd have to start hitting his meager savings account. By the end of the second week, he started reaching out to people he knew, and before long he began to pick up freelance writing assignments—P.R. releases, magazine pieces, and some newspaper stuff. It wasn't much, but it kept him afloat.

He also had an idea for a children's book. He wrote and sold it to a small publishing house. It didn't do well financially, but it boosted his ego.

After about a year and a half of successful freelancing, his old boss called him back and asked if he'd return. Though his freelancing was going well and he was hard at work on a second children's book, he accepted. But he realized that what he'd gone through wasn't so bad after all. Instead of being a problem, it was an opportunity.

Working largely at home, he cut his expenses and actually wound up increasing his income slightly. So at the end of about eighteen months, he ended up with a larger bank account than when he started, a better job, one book published, and one on the way. Oh, yes, there was the painting. He had an extra painting, too.

Story number three: This one doesn't have a happy ending, but it does offer a valuable lesson. Another person I know worked for a company that did a lot of work for the Defense Department. But in that era when defense spending was being cut back, my friend just continued on his merry way. Without knowing what was going on in his company, I asked once how things were going and if he had any concerns.

The situation he described to me seemed dire. The company put in new rules that he had to feed the Xerox machine with the clean side of papers already used once. Other people who held his position (I'm not exactly sure what he did; just that it was classified) were being let go. I could not for the life of me understand why he wasn't actively scouring the job market. I thought that even if he didn't want to switch jobs, he should at least find out what's out there. It would take someone with a psychology degree to figure out why he did (or actually didn't do) what he did.

The end of the story is that he was laid off and without a job for about three years. Ultimately he landed something with far less responsibility and far less pay. But by then he'd racked up a considerable debt, too.

The lesson here: don't allow yourself to be blindsided. Don't be in denial. Even if you think there's only a slight possibility that there will be layoffs at your company, you owe it to yourself to investigate the job market.

22

THE RIGHT JOB FOR YOU—
THE FIRST STEPS

I recently gave a class to a group of salespeople, all but one, young, aggressive, and eager to start a career. Obviously, I was intrigued by the older fellow. I'll call him George. Through no fault of his own, he was let go from his last job about a year earlier and despite his best efforts couldn't find an appropriate job. By appropriate, of course, I mean one that reflected his years on the job, the skills he'd developed, and the money he needed.

When I asked him what he wanted to do, what his expectations were for, say, the next ten years of his life, he replied that he wasn't sure; he just knew that he needed to work. So after a long and fruitless job search, he started aiming lower. Instead of continuing to investigate opportunities more fitting for someone of his age (forty-five) and experience (sales to the Defense Department), he took what is essentially an entry-level job with a manufacturer of medical equipment.

Frankly, I'm not sure why his new employer hired him. He definitely is overqualified for the job and for the pay level. If it were me doing the hiring, I'd assume (correctly) that he took the position as a stop-gap measure, until he could find something more suitable, and that it would make little sense investing in training him.

George told me that while it seemed like a good idea at the time, he was now torn about having taken this job. First of all, it left him less time to look for what he considered a permanent position. Moreover, though he was "working," he still wasn't making anywhere near enough money to support his family. And it was affecting his concentration. He wasn't getting it done at work.

I figure he has to be a great salesman, if he sold the company on himself. Getting a job is really just a matter of selling; the only difference is that now instead of trying to sell a product or service, you're selling yourself. In some ways, it should be easier, because you clearly know the product.

Selling has a process. What's the process in selling yourself to a potential new employer? Well, it starts off, as I said in the last chapter, in getting over the various funeral-like stages you go through when you lost your job: the grief, the anger, the rationalization, the bargaining with God.

The next thing you have to do—even before you start cold calling—is decide who your best prospects are. To do that you have to sit down and honestly assess where you are and where you want to go. It has to be realistic and go far beyond: I'll take this crummy job, stay for a year, and move on. Or (as one guy I know): I'm going to dye my hair so I look younger.

You may not be where you expected to be in your life, but you can't change the past. Besides, whatever vision you had of yourself twenty years ago is outdated. You can't fool yourself or anyone else. You're not twenty years old, and you likely don't have the time to accomplish what you thought you wanted twenty years ago. You've spent the last twenty, thirty, or forty years following a career path determined (or determined for you) when you were, essentially, a kid.

TIME TO RETHINK WHERE YOU'RE GOING

In real life, there was never a good time to change. You had a mortgage, you had kids, tuition, and that always meant putting yourself last. But that's probably changed or soon will. As a result, it's time you had some "me time" professionally, and by "me time" I mean now's when you should start giving more weight to your priorities.

You have to sit down and think about exactly what those priorities are and what skills you bring to the table. Ironically, from a career vantage point, this is something you should have done every year or so anyway, but few people do—until they're forced to.

Now that you fall into that latter category, now that you're forced to evaluate your professional life, you may come to realize that getting fired or laid off isn't necessarily a bad thing. On the contrary, it may be a tremendous opportunity. You could have been on a treadmill in your last job, just going through the motions. I suspect it may sound pie in the sky, but this "rejection" can actually put you back on track. At first it's really important to resist taking a job just for the sake of taking a job. Truthfully, you may wind up having to do that. But it won't make you happy, and it won't make you productive.

Ask yourself what it is that you really want to do. By that I mean, not just in your professional life, but in your personal life too. Is there a job that will bring joy to your life? What kind of company do you want to work for? Where do you want to live?

For example, let's say you're a small-town boy who's been working in the city. Perhaps you miss hunting, fishing, or just small town life. What better time to return to your roots?

Or suppose your children have moved elsewhere and you miss them and your grandchildren. Wouldn't it make you happy to find a job near them?

You also want to consider the kind of company you want to work for. Do you want to stay in the same field, or do you feel you'll be more comfortable selling something else? Might this now be a good time to start a new career? Perhaps instead of selling, you want to try life as a buyer.

Whatever you decide, it's important to remember that to be good at what you do, you must believe in what you're doing. One of the people I mentioned in a previous chapter was a car buff. So when he couldn't find work, he tried selling cars. He thought it would be the perfect transition job. The hours were such that he could continue to look for "real" work and he could make a few bucks selling a product he knew a lot about.

The problem is that he knew too much. Some of the models he sold were poorly built, had terrible crash ratings, and repair records. He couldn't bring himself to recommend them.

Is that a problem you may have had? Have you spent any time selling a product you didn't completely believe in? What are your values, and is there a company around that shares them?

Finally, whatever decision you make, will it be good for your family, your significant other, and children you may still have at home?

Making change is difficult, but if you answer these questions honestly you'll be pointed in a good direction for you—and for the company that eventually hires you. It will also speed up the process, because you won't be wasting time chasing jobs you don't want at places where you don't want to work.

Once you've pretty much settled on what it is you want, spend some time thinking about what you bring to the table. Are there specific examples of your leadership skills you can point to? Are there case histories of accounts that you have turned around? Do you have specific technological skills? What are some of the significant challenges you've faced, and how did you overcome them?

Once that's done, the next thing you need to do is your Power of Twelve—which just happens to be the subject of the next chapter.

23

THE POWER OF TWELVE

I met recently with an executive for a large recruiter. He was encountering a surprising amount of difficulty filling a CEO slot. A CEO slot, for goodness sake. He'd interviewed several dozen potential candidates, but none of them were able to separate themselves from the rest of the pack.

Now if that's happening at the CEO level, what does that make the rest of us? The reality is that—and this will likely sound terrible to you—we're all commodities, interchangeable parts in the giant wheel of commerce. But it doesn't have to be that way. You can make yourself stand out from the crowd by being smarter than everyone else. And what makes you smarter? Information.

Information is the foundation of everything we as salespeople do (or should be doing) from start to finish.

When you cold call at the beginning of the sales process, you need to know the right phone number and you need to speak to the right person. When you make an intelligent presentation at the end of the process, it has to be based on accurate information you've gathered from the prospect. In fact, those of you who know me or have read my books are aware that I believe you have to delve into a company by what I call the Power of Twelve.

That is, you need to get your primary contact to provide you access to about a dozen people in the company to help you make the sale. Ideally, you'll speak to people on the prospect company's assembly lines to find out how *your* product becomes part of the *company's* product. You'll speak to people in marketing to see how the company's product is sold. You'll need to speak to people in finance to see how it is priced.

I prefaced this by saying "ideally." You may not be able to get a dozen people to sit and talk to you. But clearly the more information you have about the prospect company and its product line, the better equipped you'll be to make a sale.

ON THE HUNT

Your job search is just an exercise in salesmanship (or saleswomanship, if you prefer). The key to success, the *Wall Street Journal* said: "Treat your (job) hunt like a business problem."

The first thing you have to do is cold call. Contact everyone you know—from colleagues to preachers, from former customers to former bosses. Be frank with them. You're looking for work. If they don't already know this about you, tell them what you've accomplished in your career. Now is not the time to be shy. Make them aware of your strengths and why you'd be a valuable addition to any staff. Do they have any leads? Do they have any ideas? Can they suggest someone you should contact? Above all, be positive.

Keep notes so you can remember whom you've met and what they said. People generally want to be helpful, but your problems and concerns can slip by the wayside in the press of everyday business. Don't be shy. Follow up on a regular basis.

Be aware of what the market is like. Check out the popular online job sites to see the number and types of positions posted. Join networking groups. If you attended chamber of commerce meetings before, don't stop now.

Don't be wed to the idea of a particular job in a particular business. Hold yourself open to every possibility. Going from selling widgets to selling Boeing aircraft is difficult, but you have to be as malleable as your product. If the prospects in your particular industry are weak, look in allied fields. Perhaps you sold your widgets to Boeing and in the process learned a great deal about the aircraft industry. Why not consider that?

First impressions

First impressions are important; the first chance you'll have to make a good one is with your resume. See a resume professional to help construct yours. "Even tiny fixes enhance a document's appeal, such as an easy-to-read format and plenty of white space," notes the *Wall Street Journal*. But content is more important than typography. Be sure your strengths are clearly stated and stand out in such a way that a prospective employer will see them clearly.

Size matters

One more point. Older salespeople regularly ask me if they should condense their resume to make them seem younger than they really are. I always argue against it for a couple of reasons. First, at some point, the person hiring you will see you. If he has problems with your age, he won't hire you. All you'll have done is waste precious time pursuing a position you're not going to get. And, yes, I know that age discrimination is illegal, but I always try to give real-world advice. Age discrimination exists.

And for the record, conversely, the most important attribute you have is your experience, so listing it all can work in your favor.

Cover letters and references

However, you can't depend on your resume alone. Every time you submit it, also include a cover letter tailored to that particular company. Cover letters have to be strong and not self-effacing.

Line up references. Be sure you're all on the same page, that they will sing exactly the praises you want sung. Check in with the references every couple of months, if your job search lasts that long, to be certain that the right message is getting out.

It's especially helpful to get a recommendation from the company that just let you go. That means, whatever happened wasn't your fault and the company would gladly take you back.

Age discrimination is certainly a reality. But the *Journal* says you can overcome it "by emphasizing . . . work ethic, dependability and experience."

INTERVIEWS

Go on every interview, even for jobs you know you'll turn down if offered. For one thing, experience will help hone your interviewing skills. For another, the person you see may have called you in for one job, but be so impressed by you that he or she winds up offering another—or suggests someone else you can contact.

THE BRIDGE BEHIND YOU MAY END UP IN FRONT OF YOU—SO DON'T BURN IT!

Don't burn bridges. The writer friend of mine I mentioned in a previous chapter felt he was fired unjustly. At the good-bye party thrown in his honor he let out all the venom that built up in his system over the previous weeks out. After pointing out that in the previous months a number of veterans of the company—people who'd been with publishing company for a decade and more—were summarily let go. He wondered what happened to corporate loyalty, concluding with three simple words: "This company sucks." My friend was fortunate in two respects. First he never intended to go back to work for that company, and second he hadn't burned bridges with his previous employer, who gladly took him back (after making him sweat a couple of months).

As the *Journal* points out, it's difficult to keep from feeling despair. More than eighteen percent of the people unemployed have been so for at least twenty-seven weeks. And obviously the longer you are without work, the worse you feel. But confidence is an ally.

24

Landing the Interview

There are times when someone scans the help-wanted ads in the *Wall Street Journal* or a large metropolitan area newspaper, and finds a sales job that seems perfect for them. The money and commissions are better than just right. The product is a leader in its field. And the company is one you've always wanted to work for with great benefits and a good attitude toward its people. The only thing wrong with the ad is that it doesn't say "Only (insert your name) should apply."

Yes, there are occasions when that happens, when all the stars are aligned right about the time of the dawning of the Age of Aquarius. In fact, if my memory serves me correctly I believe the last time a job hunt went down like that was 1966. The reality is that online job postings and newspaper ads are not the best way to find work—especially at a more senior level. You have a better chance of finding a job through contacts and a network of acquaintances.

Responding to a help-wanted ad

If you see the perfect job advertised, you don't want to blindly send in a resume. Use all the resources at your disposal to find out what company placed the ad. Better still, if you can, discover who is doing the hiring. If the job is that good you may be competing with hundreds of applicants, so use any advantage you have.

Become a CSI investigator. The crime is that you're out of work and need a job, so you have to sift through all the clues. If you figure out the company's name, check your Rolodex to see if you know anyone who currently works there or perhaps someone who recently left. See if they can help you find out who'll be doing the hiring. Don't respond to a blind box number ad. Send your resume directly to him or her.

If your spy knows the person and says it's okay, use her name. "Jane Smith thought I'd be the perfect candidate for the sales position you are trying to fill." If that doesn't work and there's no one's name you can use, just say that you understand that the prospect is looking for a position, and that you are uniquely qualified to fill the post. Then list your reasons and say you'll call to set up an appointment. If nothing else, it's likely that the prospect will be impressed with your initiative. It will immediately set you apart from the rest of the applicants who simply sent in a resume.

USING THE NETWORK

The chances are, however, that your next job will come from networking, not a newspaper or online advertisement. You've told everyone you know about the kind of position you're looking for. They've provided all the information at their disposal and suggested other folks you should contact. Your seeds are planted and some fruit comes back to you in the form of potential job leads.

You do everything by the book. You have a spiffy resume that highlights your expertise, and you have written a cover letter tailored specifically to this company's needs. You send them off and wait.

Don't. Your resume and cover letter, no matter how good they are, will not carry you. Now's the time for you to pick up the telephone and make a call. But be prepared.

An irony of this business is that salespeople and managers frequently treat people trying to sell to them like dirt. Without flinching, they'll do unto others the very things they do not want done unto them.

Remember that guy I met on a flight, the one who is a sales vice president for a large international printing company?

He gave me his e-mail address and suggested I contact him when I got back to my office. I want to repeat that: *He gave me his e-mail address and suggested I contact him when I got back to my office!*

You already know the end of this story. He never got back to me. I was tempted to send him a nasty note and tell him what I thought of him. But what was the point? Here was a guy who suggested I call him. Who told me he'd call back. Who at any point in the process could have said, "Look, Steve, when I got back to the office I found our budget was shot," or "I bounced it off my boss and he's just not interested," or "I'm a stupid idiot and I never should have encouraged you." Well, maybe not the last one.

I understand that people are busy and that hiring me to deliver my course may not have been his highest priority. I know, too, that he may have run into some kind of buzz saw when he got back to his office, a series of crises that kept him from responding to my e-mail. But clearly that was not the case here.

What would he be feeling if a potential client treated him in the same way? I'm sure he'd be angry, too. I mention this because you are going to be down on yourself while you are out of work. This may be the first time in your life that you have been unemployed. The last thing you are going to need in your life is encountering some self-absorbed (expletive-deleted) who is not concerned about the way you feel.

But you will run into far more of them than people like me. I make it a practice to return every call and be honest with sales callers. It is fundamentally important for you to keep in mind that the fact that they don't return your calls or e-mails is a reflection on them, not on you. You cannot work yourself up over it. All you can do is move on.

COLD CALLING A POTENTIAL EMPLOYER

This brings me back to networking. You receive no response to the cover letter and resume that you sent. So you call and don't get through. If that happens several times over the first week or two that you try, see above: Move on. Get over it.

But since you are using an acquaintance's name to gain access to the prospect, the chances are you'll get some kind of response. At some point, you will get through or she will return your call. What do you do then?

First of all, you have to stay focused on your mission. You want to make the case that you still have a viable sales career and that you are not just looking for a job. You are looking for a position that will allow you to use your expertise.

And use that expertise in making this phone call. "Ms. Smith, we have a mutual friend, Bill Jones. He suggested I send you a resume using him as a reference. I sent it to you about a week ago, and I'm wondering if you've had a chance to read it yet."

Based on your experience, you know that there are only a few possible answers to this question, and you're prepared for them all. If she says yes, she's read it, you ask if you can tell her a little more about your pertinent experience. If she says no, she hasn't read it, you ask, "Well, can I briefly describe my pertinent experience?" And if she says, yes, she's read it, but there's no opening at the moment, you say, "I was afraid that might be the case. But if you'll give me just a second, I'd like to tell you about my experience and why I think it might be worthwhile for us to get together."

In each of these examples, it's your job to make clear your experience, how that experience meshes with that company's product line, and customers. And somewhere during this call, you must say, "I think I have some ideas that will substantially help your company."

As I've said many times over the years, when it comes to sales there are two important words: idea and imagine. Both create a vision of possibilities in the mind's eye of the person you are speaking to. When you've created that vision, suggest a time and date to meet.

Never say, "What time is good for you?" That will give her a chance to counter with, "There really is no good time." But if you've done a good job, and the time you suggest is not right for her, she'll likely make a counter proposal, "No, that's no good. How about Wednesday at 11?"

A couple of things you don't want to say in a phone call or in a subsequent meeting:

1. "I'm looking for a position that challenges me." What does that mean? It's the kind of jargon that is just as likely to turn off a prospective boss as it to interest him. An applicant may want to reinvent themselves, yes, but not as a completely different person. Instead, say you're looking for a position that will allow you to use the skills, wisdom, and experience you gained over the years.

2. Don't brag about quotas you've met and awards you've won. It's unseemly. Besides, you've probably listed them in your resume, anyway.

25

THE INTERVIEW

One of the difficulties in writing any self-improvement or how-to book is that the writer—me—can only talk in generalities about the reader—you. And you. And you. In real life, every one of us is different and every situation is different.

So what I've tried to do is synthesize for you the most common situations and hope that you can take something from my suggestions to adapt to your particular situation. However, there are a few rules that are universal, and apply to everyone no matter his or her situation:

1. Do not set yourself up to be a loser. That is, don't take a job just for the sake of having a job. Don't put yourself in a situation where you will fail because you took employment that was not right for your skill set, your temperament, or for your station in life. Because if you do, it will set you up for failure. And failure can become a pattern and a reputation.

2. Don't act as though you're on a job interview. You are on a sales mission, and the product you are selling is you. Once you understand that, it's easier to draw on your past experience. You know that this isn't a quick one-shot deal; this is a process. You'll likely have to sell

yourself to more than one individual. Don't get frustrated. Think back to a big sale that took you months and months to close.

3. Use the skills you have to build rapport. It's fine to talk about the experience you have and the great relationships you've built with customers over the years. I usually begin by saying, "Would it help if I told you something about me?" The response you get almost always is positive. Don't brag. On the contrary, be modest about your achievements. Leave it to your references to tell what a great salesperson you are.

4. Ask questions. Get your prospect involved in a conversation. What is it she expects of the person she hires? How does the company sell now? Who had the job before? What did he or she do right? What did he or she do wrong?

5. Give examples. I recently ran an ad for a salesman and got literally hundreds of resumes. I lost count of how many people I interviewed, but all of them said they could do the job. Poppycock. Don't say you can do the job. Give examples of something similar you've done. Better still, demonstrate a methodology that is superior.

6. See if you can discern the culture of the company. There is a conflict in selling philosophy at many companies. Top management wants to put the sales force into teams. We're a team here, they say; selling is a team sport. I did some work for a company where selling was a blood sport. The salespeople competed against each other. As I investigated the firm so I could tailor a course for it, I worked my way up the ladder and eventually had a meeting with the founder. He has "Executioner" as his title of his business card, and he kept piranhas in his office. Better to find that out early on, especially if that's not an environment you can prosper in.

7. Even if it turns out that this is not a job for you, keep going and selling. There may be another job, perhaps even a bigger opportunity, at the company for you. Perhaps, based on your experience and the

impression you make, the prospect will talk to you about a management position. Or she might know of a position that better fits your skill set at another company where she knows the sales director. In short: Never stop selling.

8. No matter what the company is, dress conservatively—even if you are selling to Google or one of the dotcoms where everyone comes to work in shorts or jeans. You'll have plenty of time to dress down once you're hired.

9. Never say anything about yourself, even as a joke, which can be interpreted negatively. I had a young man come in for a job who told me that his current position was all about numbers. So he started taking business cards from the fishbowl at the diner and representing those as people he's met with. I liked him and maybe it showed. In retrospect, I think that's why he trusted me sufficiently to tell that story. But I knew at that moment I could never hire him because I could never trust him. Similarly, I know of a case where a job applicant bragged about something he'd done to close a big sale. It wasn't illegal, but it straddled the line that separates ethical from immoral. He believed what he was saying would be viewed positively. It would show him as a man who'd go to any lengths to clinch a sale. In fact, this company doesn't operate that way, and he was never called back for another interview.

10. Listen. Your prospect will give you hints about how to get this job and how you're doing. If she says we're looking for someone who has experience selling widgets and you do, say so. Even if you don't, you might have experience selling another product to the same people who buy widgets—meaning you have contacts in the field.

Closing the interview

How do you close the interview? The idea is (just as in sales) to get to the next step, whatever they may be. You might say, "Would it be helpful if I met with other members of your team?" Or: "This really sounds like a great company and a great opportunity. I'll start tomorrow if you let me."

In either case you'll get a reaction. In some cases it will be positive and (depending where you are in the process) you will be hired. Or you will be asked to meet with someone else in the company.

But it could also be that the answer is negative. Don't give up immediately. Don't say "okay" and slink out with your tail between your legs. Say, "I'm disappointed. I'd hoped to work for this company, and I thought I'd made a pretty good case for myself. Where did I slip up?" Put the onus on the prospect. If he rethinks everything you've told him, perhaps he'll rethink response to you. In any event, what have you got to lose?

For our purposes, however, we're going to assume you got the job and in the next chapter talk about your first days in a new office.

26

YOUR NEW JOB

No matter how many times you've done it, no matter how old you are, starting a new job is always a little nerve wracking. Even if you know some of the people at your new place of business, you're still the outsider, the unknown, the potential threat to your new coworkers' commissions. This is doubly true if you are the mature salesperson. While some of the younger guys may roll their eyes and automatically assume you are a dinosaur, the smarter ones will understand that in an increasingly competitive marketplace, no manager hires a relic just for the sake of having a body in the office. Not only are you probably a good salesperson, but based on your experience you make have been able to work out a better financial package than they have.

In either case, you are walking on potential landmines that can explode and make this job very uncomfortable for you. Or you can skirt the mines. Doing the latter is relatively easy. Most of what you need to do is obvious.

1. Treat your colleagues in a professional manner. Don't come on gangbusters as God's gift to sales. Use your people skills.

2. You may have been hired as a company effort to upgrade the sales staff. That's between you and management. Don't be braggadocio. Ultimately, you need to become part of a team, so it's important that

you don't create a situation that confirms the impression that you're an outsider.

3. Don't bring in every sales award you ever won and put them on your desk or wall or any place where people can see them. You're starting in a new place. It's a blank slate. What you did in the past is meaningless here—except insofar as it will arouse resentment.

4. Don't bring in photos of you playing golf with the president (of the company or the United States). See three above.

5. Make every effort to become part of the group. If you're invited out to lunch with the gang, go—even if you've brown bagged it that day or everyone is going to a Chinese restaurant and you're allergic to MSG.

6. Conversely, don't be the person who always pays for drinks in an ill-disguised attempt to purchase popularity.

7. Show a willingness to mentor. Don't push yourself on new colleagues, but if someone asks for a suggestion or help, put aside what you are doing and provide it. It may mean you have to work a little later that day or come in earlier the next, but you will reap substantial benefits.

8. If you overhear someone describing a problem that you've dealt with before, wait until you see them alone to offer your expertise.

9. Be open to ideas from your coworkers. Listen to what they have to say. You never know where the next great sales idea will come from.

10. You do not know it all. I recently attended a seminar where a successful woman sales manager described to a group of mostly younger salespeople the way she encourages her employees to sell. But there was one older guy in the back who kept mumbling to himself throughout most of the presentation, until the presenter couldn't take it any more. "What's the problem?" she asked the guy.

He said, "You can't do it that way." This know-it-all was telling a successful sales manager that she couldn't do the very things that had made her a success. Don't be that guy.

11. Note that I said I attended this seminar, not that I gave it. You should attend sales training courses as often as possible. After all these years, I'm still open to sales training, in part because I know I do not know it all. Also, being around a lot of young salespeople when I'm not the one lecturing is refreshing. I almost always get at least one idea for my courses from them.

12. Like a lot of salespeople, you may be working in a virtual office from your home. Because of all your experience, you know a lot of ways to cut corners. Don't. There's not anything necessarily wrong with cutting corners, but knowing you can do so creates a negative mentality. You don't have to get up until nine in the morning and you need work only until four in the afternoon. Not only do you have to resist the impulse to say what the heck, you probably ought to be working harder to reestablish your bona fides.

THE NEW BOSS

Let's talk a little bit now about your new sales manager, who may—or may not—be the person who actually hired you. Do not transfer to him or her any ill feelings you've had toward previous managers. Remember, it's a clean slate. In the same way that you want people to accept you with an open mind, you need to extend that same courtesy to your new manager.

27

Meeting Expectations

Why do you think you were hired? There are any number of interesting scenarios:

- The company unsuccessfully has been trying to land a major new account. Management feels your experience can make a difference.
- The company is in the midst of significant expansion. Management feels your experience can make the difference.
- The company is introducing a new product line. Management feels your experience can make the difference.

That you got the job means two things. First of all, you're a good salesperson. You sold yourself, your experience, and your capabilities. Second, the person who hired you bought it. The manager almost certainly could have hired someone else, perhaps someone else with less experience (requiring a less remunerative commission agreement), but she chose you. That's the good news.

The bad news is that you did so good a job that you set up high expectations—perhaps unrealistically high. You're the guy. You're the one who will get the sale no one else has been able to. You'll know how to reach the unreachable customer. The question then is: Do you become Don Quixote and tilt at windmills, or do you take a more realistic approach?

It can be daunting and add a significant amount of pressure to your life at exactly the time you don't want extra pressure. You've been through a lot lately, ranging from the middle-age blahs to an unexpected job search.

In a perfect world, you'd have an opportunity to ease into your new job. But we know the world isn't perfect. Your manager is going to expect you to meet his expectations—and quickly. Depending upon the kind of office it is and the kind of people who are your coworkers, they may actually be hoping for you to fail.

SET PRACTICAL GOALS WITH YOUR MANAGER

You may very well be able to come into a new company all gangbusters and immediately generate scads of business. This works most often when you go to work for a competitor of your previous employer and are able to bring some of your client base with you. But even that doesn't happen quickly, because most of your former clients are contractually tied to your former company—at least for a while.

Where does that leave you? First of all, you have to be realistic and set a realistic outlook for your manager. There isn't a salesperson in the world who doesn't shoot for signing up the Big Elephant, that one big sale that can define a career.

And this is where your experience comes into play. Some kid might run willy-nilly into the elephant and probably get smacked in the head by its trunk. You, on the other hand, know that there are no magic cannons in sales. You can't bring down an elephant with one shot.

To mix my metaphor, don't go after the whole enchilada. You have to go after it pieces at a time, division by division, region by region, one sale leading to another until the elephant is yours. You may have to convince a young sales manager that you're correct.

The best way to do that is to start nibbling at the elephant (or enchilada, if you prefer). Meanwhile, in the rest of the game (not to add a sports metaphor to the mix) be a high-average singles hitter. Go after smaller accounts that will raise your batting average—not to mention your prestige in the office.

Initially, I was going to devote a sizable section of this book to the sales process—prospecting, initial meetings, the Power of Twelve, and presentations. But I soon realized that was likely a waste of your time and a good forest. If you need to review the sales process, I have a dozen or so books to recommend. (And, for the record, they're all written by me.)

Besides, the basic premise of this book is that you are a good salesperson and you've just reached a crossroad in your life. You're just at that point where you still feel like a kid, but realize you aren't one anymore. Your new job, however, is really a great opportunity. There's a great deal of pressure on you, but you're facing a blank slate. You have the opportunity to start a whole new life, a rebirth if you will.

But best of all, you know so much more than you did the first time you were born. I imagine there are one or two people on the globe who look back at their lives without regrets. But I think most of us have told ourselves at one time or another we'd like to go back and live portions of our lives over again—but knowing what we know. Well, that's what you're doing with this new job. You're reliving your professional youth.

*Peter Georgescu is the former CEO and chairman emeritus
of Young & Rubicam advertising agency.*

Probably a fair proportion of younger people in the business world look at older folks as dinosaurs. But I believe the issue is less one of age, than the lack of willingness of some people to change, to keep up to date, to stay relevant. They automatically consider an older person out of it.

But I think that's a function of mindset, willingness to understand the ever-changing environment around them, the new factors that drive the business world and the economy. I'm certainly an aging warrior; the question is do I bring something to the party? The issue isn't age or years on the job but do I have the ability to help people drive the business forward.

There are young people who come into the picture who don't know what the heck they're talking about. By the same token, wrinkles on the face don't mean the person is knowledgeable. Through experience I've learned to discern pretty quickly if a person is worth listening to.

A young employee at Y&R once came into my office trying to convince me to invest in a business. She came in with a business plan that showed how revenues were still growing, but profits were nowhere in sight. She believed in the "r" word, revenue and felt the "p" word was irrelevant. I told her you can't work that way. She said to me, "Mr. Georgescu, you're too old."

I wasn't upset by that comment. Her pimples showed a lack of wisdom.

PART VII

YOUR CAREER PATH

28

MENTORING

I predict you will be a great in your new position. I also predict that no matter what they thought of you the first time you walked through the office door, your younger colleagues will soon come to you for advice. They will if they're smart, for a couple of reasons.

First, as you rapidly fill your book and sign clients, you will clearly demonstrate your expertise. Furthermore, you are a great alternative to going to the sales manager with problems. Needing help implies weakness, and that is not something a young salesperson wants to reveal to the boss.

As we shall see, mentoring is a win-win situation for everyone. So while this chapter is ostensibly directed at senior sales people starting a new job, there are benefits that sales folk long established at their companies can gain, too.

HOW DO YOU GET INTO MENTORING?

There is no single path to mentoring. Over the course of time at your new job, you develop relationships with your new coworkers. You'll like and get close to some more than others, and some will like you more than others. You'll all go out to lunch or dinner together or perhaps drinks after work. And then it happens. Trying to describe it would be like my trying to explain how you meet the person you will marry or who will become your significant other. It just happens.

In fact, for it to work there has to be chemistry between the two of you. Many companies have set up mentoring programs, but many if not most of them fail. Because—I know I've said this before, and I will undoubtedly say this again—while people like to talk about a sales "team," sales is really an individual sport.

You have to be willing to advise and help someone who may become a competitor somewhere down the line. You have to be willing to give up your secrets, those techniques and short cuts you've developed over the years. That's asking a lot, and it won't happen if there isn't a special something between the two of you.

The mentee is also subtly giving up a bit of his or her independence. No one, but especially cocky young salespeople, likes to admit they need help.

WHY GET INTO MENTORING?

Mentoring is a win-win situation. That your younger colleagues come to you for advice means they have come to respect and trust you. Not only do they believe you can help them, but they trust you will not run to the boss and reveal what they tell you. That's an important hurdle to overcome.

Moreover, mentoring has a positive effect on you. It is a way to regain your spirit and enthusiasm for selling. In many ways you can learn as much as you teach; watching and listening to your mentee is a way to recapture the fervor you once felt and a reminder of the way you once sold.

Also, mentoring is payback. In all likelihood, someone mentored you and this is your effort to keep the positive cosmic karma going, passing along the wisdom that was given to you.

But the truth of the matter, too, is it's probably also a little bit of an ego trip. That is, we tend to mentor our clones. We're attracted to people we believe are our mirror images from twenty or thirty years ago. Nurturing them, guiding them through rough spots, giving back makes mentors feel good. But it does more than that. It reminds us of what we used to be like and how we used to sell. I think that makes us better salespeople, too.

A FEW CAUTIONARY NOTES ABOUT MENTORING

But conversely, because we all know that no good deed goes unpunished, there are a couple of slightly negative side effects of mentoring. For example, some colleagues may be offended by your new role, or by the fact that you don't give them as much time as they would like.

Another potential problem is the boss, who might also resent and feel a little threatened by the special bond building between two of his salespeople. A rule of thumb is that sales managers are supposed to spend about half their time mentoring and otherwise aiding their staffs. In truth, because of administrative and other duties, their schedules are such that they're lucky to spend twenty percent of the time doing the part of the job they probably like best.

But these are relatively inconsequential problems, because they'll really only arise if you somehow flaunt what you're doing. If you're discreet, these shouldn't be obstacles to mentoring. In fact, a wise sales manager will appreciate your mentoring for obvious reasons. It relieves a burden from his or her shoulders and improves his or her group's performance. Mentoring makes you a more valuable member of the team.

The only significant downside to mentoring (other than the possibility that the person you mentor turns out to be a complete jerk) is that it is an additional demand on your time. Selling is about using time efficiently and wisely; there's never enough time in the day. You don't get paid to be a mentor, and there's a risk that mentoring might take too much time that might be more profitably spent on cultivating your own sales.

So for mentoring to work you have to set up parameters. The mentee can't just approach you willy-nilly in the office while you're working, interrupting your concentration and thought process. There have to be rules set up. Perhaps you discuss problems only over a regularly scheduled lunch or after work.

No matter how you work it out, it is usually a positive experience. I have mentored several people over the course of my career. While it is perhaps an overstatement to say that these were the greatest experiences I've had—Big Sales I've closed make up that category—it is right up there in terms of the pleasure and satisfaction it's given me.

29

Becoming a Manager

Let's suppose you get interviewed by the senior sales executive for a company that you would love to work for. You pull out all the stops. You wow her. You know you've hit this one out of the park. Mickey Mantle, Hank Aaron, Roger Maris, and all the great long ball hitters who did it without chemical enhancements are jealous of this interview.

Then the aforementioned senior sales executive throws you a curve ball. "I'm really impressed with what you said today. Unfortunately, I think you're overqualified for the sales job."

Your heart sinks, and then she adds, "But I believe you'd make a perfect manager for our widget group." (Again, the rationale behind this chapter applies equally to salespeople who stay at the same job.)

Your heart does not recover. If you were as good a salesperson as I suspect you were, you probably have been offered management jobs before. My guess is that you turned them down. And I wish I could argue with your logic. For some salespeople, management is the pot of gold at the end of the rainbow. But for a lot of us the negatives far outweigh the ego gratification that comes from being able to say, "I'm a sales manager," when you've been used to introducing yourself as a sales "person."

Is it time for a change of heart?

Has anything changed? Is now the time you should reconsider your anti-management bias? These aren't easy questions to answer because there are so many variables—in your personality and in the culture of the various companies that may hire you. So what to do?

First of all, understand what being a manager means. For one thing, it means more politics. It's hard to avoid that. The higher up you travel on the corporate ladder, the thinner the air and the greater the political intensity.

You are also going to wind up doing a lot more paperwork and general administrative work. As a salesperson, you might have to attend regular meetings with your manager. But as a manager, you must meet regularly with your sales force *and* your managers. You have to set budgets. You need to hire people. You need to fire people.

You may actually miss sales. If you're a road warrior, you may long for the time you used to spend on the road.

And the straw that may break the camel's back: Not only may you wind up earning less money, but what you do earn will largely be dependent upon others.

Managing is not for everyone. I know (in hindsight) that I was terrible at it when I first started—for two reasons, I think. First, a lot of my experience as a salesman was working for managers who were beyond awful, concerned only with the short term sales (and bonuses) rather than taking a longer view. Secondly, I was too young. I believe I didn't have enough sales experience to successfully manage a sales force.

But I blindly felt my way forward, learned from my mistakes, and over a period of time got better at it.

I don't mean to paint too negative a picture of management. While your earnings may be less than what you earned as a salesperson—do a good job and you could bring home substantially more greenbacks than you thought possible. Do a good job and you may even get promoted to higher ranks.

In the last chapter, we discussed your role as a salesperson/mentor. Here mentoring (and all the good feelings that come with it) is actually part of your job. And you don't need to limit it to one person. Your entire sales crew will have an opportunity to benefit from your experience. And that's another point. I was twenty-seven when I took my first management job. You're . . . well, you know how old you are. Your wisdom and maturity level will likely enable you to do a much better job than I did.

HOW TO MAKE A CHOICE

Ultimately, though, you're the only one who can decide whether or not to take a management position. You have to weigh your personality. You also want to consider what other options you have. And you have to decide whether you believe that management can provide you the same level of satisfaction that you received from sales.

If you decide that you may be interested in the position, you're going to need some additional information. Presumably you've done your homework and are familiar with the company and its culture. It is a place you want to work. Obviously, you want to find out what you'll be paid and what your benefits and perks will be.

But, more importantly, you need to get what is expected of you clearly laid out. You need to find out what responsibilities you have and whether or not you will have the authority to fulfill them. Will you be able to hire and fire, if necessary? What kind of hoops will you have to jump through to add or subtract personnel? How does senior management see the sales manager's position? Do they want the manager to be a mentor or an administrator?

As the negotiations become more serious and detailed, you have every right to ask what happened to the previous manager. How does senior management evaluate the personnel you'll be handled? Has there been substantial turnover in the department?

The chances are that the company is going to want a reasonably swift decision from you. But obviously that's not something you can give. The first thing to do is say, "Wow. That caught me a little off guard. I need some time to think this through."

You don't need time to think this through as much as you need time to verify the information you've been given. Obviously, if the info turns out to be incorrect, this is not the job for you. Ultimately, based on everything you've learned, it's up to you to decide if you want the *job*. I emphasize the word job, because the package shouldn't factor into your thinking. They can promise you Really Big Bucks, but if it's a job you don't like, you won't do it well. And then pretty soon you'll be out on the street earning unemployment insurance. Remember what I said earlier: never agree to be a loser. If you take a job just for the sake of having a job, that's what you'll be.

Your first days as manager

But if you decide to take the position, there is a definite action plan you have to follow:

1. Win over your salespeople. Have a meeting the first day on the job to introduce yourself. Meet with each salesperson individually, and give them an opportunity to air their grievances. Almost always, the people on the front lines have a better idea of what's right—and, more importantly, what's wrong—with an organization. You can learn more about what is going on in the company from your salespeople than you will from your management.

2. Take your time setting ground rules and laying down the law.Learn about your salespeople and the environment they work in. You can best spend your early time in management as an advocate for your people. If someone has a legitimate complaint about the way he's been treated, go to bat for him or her. Get it straightened out, and you will an instant ally for life.

3. Push for your group, but not so hard that you alienate other sales managers in the corporation. They can sabotage your success.

4. As soon as possible, let your bosses know what your plans are, which of course means that you . . .

5. Have a plan. Let the bosses know how you expect to accomplish your mission in as short a time as possible. Every new sales manager gets a honeymoon period—that is a time when they can think about and formulate what they are going to do. But the honeymoon is usually over long before the bosses said it would end. Example: I tried to sell a program to the newly appointed sales manager of a large division of a large corporation. I'd worked with him before, so I figured this would be a no-brainer. But he told me he just started. He'd been given six months to develop his plan and think things through. He didn't want to rush things. Three weeks later he called and said he had to set up a training program immediately. It turned out his boss promised six months but meant six weeks. The new sales manager should have known better. In today's economy, no company is going to give a new sales manager half a year to find himself. When you come up with a plan be sure to . . .

6. Go on a call with each salesperson. Let her pick the account. Presumably, she'll pick an account she has a good relationship with. That's fine. Watching her interact with a customer—even a friend—provides a substantial glimpse into her abilities. But make it clear you'll be visiting troubled accounts with her as well.

7. Don't rock the boat right away. I've seen too many sales managers come in, decide they like the power, and start grandstanding for the bosses in the hope of winning further promotions. Get a feeling for who's who and what's what before you do something that will come back and bite you.

30

BECOMING A CONSULTANT

Over the course of your sales career you've built up substantial expertise in a number of areas. Although you may not have followed the principles I teach to the letter, you hopefully have done something similar to achieve your success.

The bedrock of what I teach is about information. To be a good salesperson, you have to know your product backward and forward. No one should know more about what you sell than you do. And here I'm not referring specifically to the technical specifications of, say widgets. I mean widgets' malleability. You have to know how your product can be modified to meet the specialized needs of your customers.

That also requires you to know your customers. If you're familiar with my books or courses (or read previous chapters of this one), you know that I advocate a system I call the Power of Twelve. That is, after you meet with a prospect for the first time, you say something like, "I'd like to come back to you with a proposal based on our discussion. But I really want it to be well thought out and intelligent. So, what I'd like to do is meet some more people from the company: someone in your engineering department, someone who works in the factory, perhaps a salesman and someone from your marketing department. This will allow me to get a fuller picture of how my widgets are used and enable me to construct a smarter presentation."

By the time you were through researching you probably knew more about the company or at least that division than the CEO did. In effect, if you were selling properly. You were acting as a consultant for this company, advising them how to get a product at a lower price delivered where and when they want it.

So why not do it full time?

WHERE YOU ARE NOW

Let's examine your situation. You've been selling for more than two decades. You've got the blahs, and your job doesn't excite you the way it once did.

We've spent much of the last hundred or so pages talking about the way you can rejuvenate your career. But realistically that may not be the answer. You are probably vested in your pension/retirement plan. Perhaps now is the time to move on. (Of course, if you've been laid off you may not have a choice.) But certainly becoming a consultant is a viable alternative.

But it isn't an easy transition. Going from a regular pay check to being out on your own is frightening. Before you make that leap, here are some of the issues (many mundane, but also many overlooked) you have to examine:

1. Getting your own business up and running often is an expensive investment. From little things such as letterhead and business cards to buying computers, printers, and other hard- and software, startup costs can take a big bite out of your savings.

2. How long will you be able to survive without a paycheck? Even if you get started with a client or two, it can be several months before you get your first paycheck.

3. The devil is in the details. Have you made arrangements for medical insurance? Have you checked with an accountant on what's the most advantageous way to set up your consulting company?

4. Are you sure you're mentally tough enough to make this transition? You've been a salesperson for twenty or more years. You're used to being out among people. Presumably, at first, you'll run this company out of your home. It can be overbearingly lonely and depressing. There's the constant temptation to go up and raid the refrigerator or become a fan of *As the World Turns*. I've found that people who set up consultancies often lack the discipline and focus to finish the assignments they have. They stay up late, don't start work in anywhere near a timely manner, and generally act like school kids, pulling an all-nighter before a big exam or a report is due.

5. You have to treat it as a business. Too often, "consultant" is a euphemism for "unemployed." You need to make it clear to potential clients that this isn't something to keep you busy until you find a "real" job. This is your real job. And you pretty much have to be in it for the long haul. The longer you are a consultant, the more difficult it may become to go back into a salaried position. Human resource people seem to eye consultants suspiciously. Once you've spent any time out of the corporate mainstream, they're reluctant to let you back in.

6. Modern technology allows you to work anywhere, including from the local coffee shop. But you really have to stock up on all the accoutrements of a real office: desks, filing cabinets, and you need a place to put them. The most important piece of furniture you'll need is a solid door, one that will keep your spouse, your kids, your dog and cat out. They have to understand that though you're home, you are really at work and are not to be disturbed.

7. Just because you became a consultant doesn't mean you gave up selling. I wrote a book called *The Consultant's Handbook,* and the

thing I emphasized there is that you can't spend all your time working as a consultant. Even if you have more business than you think you can handle, you need to set part of your time for selling. You must continue to chase the next piece of business. Of course, the best part of this equation is that it's your piece of business you're chasing. You're not selling for someone else's profit.

IT'S UP TO YOU NOW

Michael Gates Gill wrote *How Starbucks Saved My Life,* a book I really loved and is entirely appropriate for our discussion. Gill was a senior executive for over two decades with a large advertising agency. At age fifty-three, he was fired, he believes, because the agency's new owner considered him too old. He never filed a formal complaint, because the agency promised to funnel some consulting his way. And it did. For a while. But over the course of a couple of years, personnel changed. The people who gave him business moved on and their replacements didn't take his calls. And before long there was no business anymore. Though he doesn't say so in the book, my guess is that Gill didn't make the effort he should to sell new clients.

On the other hand, starting your own business can be an exhilarating and very profitable experience. But as with everything else we've discussed in this book, you need to approach consulting with confidence. If you do not believe that the experience and wisdom you've built up is valuable, you won't be able to convince potential clients of it. Take stock of yourself. Realize how good you really are!

31

CHANGING CAREERS

Frankly, this is not a chapter I wanted to write. I am a sales trainer by profession. I am not a get-out-of-sales-trainer. But the reality is that we're all living longer. Most of us have a variety of interests and options at our fingertips that were not even dreamed of by our parents—cable television, the computer, a telephone we actually carry with us. The point is we now have access to a number of different careers and the extra lifetime to enjoy them. Maybe it really is time to give up sales.

You have to decide if you still have to work or you work because you want to. Remember Gill from the last chapter, the one who wrote *How Starbucks Saved My Life*. He was a graduate of Yale, an obviously bright guy, but one now completely down and out. He didn't know where his next dollar was coming from. But he walked into a Starbucks for a cup of coffee, when a store manager asked him if he'd be interested in a job. He doesn't know what possessed him to say yes, but he did. And he soon found himself behind the counter making coffee. And, as he writes, he took particular pleasure in keeping the restroom clean.

MONEY ISN'T EVERYTHING

It sounds strange, but I know someone who did almost the same thing. He was the head of a large buying co-op for independent pharmacies.

He made several hundred thousand dollars a year and had a lot of perks, including a big expense account and company car. But somewhere in his fifties, he just got tired of it. He had all the money he'd ever need, so he quit and took a job as a stock boy. He worked for a candy company and went from supermarket to supermarket stocking shelves with the company's products. He probably made little more than the minimum wage, but that wasn't the point. He just wanted to be happy.

If you are at midlife and have been so successful that you don't *need* to work anymore, then the world is your oyster. And this oyster is filled with pearls, jobs that will allow you to tap into skills you never thought you had before, jobs that provide a sense of satisfaction you didn't get in sales, and jobs that will just keep you busy. If you can look into the future and say, "Look, I have more than enough for my spouse and I to live a decent lifestyle for the next thirty or forty years. Why shouldn't I spend that time doing something that brings me joy?"

MONEY MAY NOT BE EVERYTHING, BUT IT'S BETTER THAN NOTHING

But the reality is that most of us need to work. And more often than not, the jobs we want to do don't pay enough money. In sales, we're not always seen as experts. But we are. And you likely have an impressive resume that will be welcome in a number of different industries and jobs. Another possibility is buying a franchise. Generally that's the safest, most proven way of going into business for yourself.

Whatever you do, remember you are a person who has demonstrated the skills to build business. You've sold to accounts no one else could. You've kept book for years. You are a miracle worker who has skills that apply to whatever you do.

Whatever you do!

32

IN THE BEGINNING

In the beginning, there was this young salesman. Let's call him Jim, for simplicity's sake. Jim got into sales, found he had an affinity for it, and prospered. He got married and had a family, but around the age of forty things started to seem off kilter.

Selling didn't hold the same appeal it once did. Going to work wasn't the pleasure it once was. It became a chore. Jim found himself dealing with younger people who didn't respect him or his experience and wisdom. *They* knew it all and viewed Jim as a dinosaur, a relic of some long-forgotten age.

In one way or another, if you are reading this book—and have gotten this far—I think each of us can identify with Jim. Most of us feel as young as we did when we were kids. So it comes as something of a shock to look in the mirror and unexpectedly see your mother or father staring back at you. Or suddenly realize that your children, who were just born a few months ago—are actually graduating from high school or college.

I can't give you a scientific reason for why or when this occurs, but there are moments in time when you suddenly realize the dreams you had growing up just aren't going to happen, or you get bored with your job or any number of other things. I know it all sounds depressing, but it happens.

My goal in writing this book was to prepare you for this, assure you that what's happened or is happening to you is not unique to you, and to try to help you get past it.

The idea for this book germinated with the call about five years ago I described in Chapter One. But it was nurtured over the last several years as the Baby Boomers I coached began telling me stories about how they couldn't stand their jobs, or they couldn't get up the energy to go to work anymore. At first, I dismissed the complaints. But they became more common. And pretty soon, I didn't wait for someone to bring the topic up. I brought it up myself.

What I found was that while not everyone resented or had problems at work, everyone had problems. While I'd heard and read about middle-age crisis, I'd never seen it demonstrated so clearly. It seemed to be everywhere. Though, truth be told, maybe I just noticed it more because I was beginning to feel it, as well.

I decided I was going to try to figure out how to avoid the blahs—I call it that because "middle-age crisis" sounds so undignified—and to a certain extent I did. At least for me. And it is those tips I wanted to impart here.

YOU'RE NOT ALONE

As I noted previously, midway in the writing for this book, scientists on two continents revealed the results of a study that apparently most people on the Planet Earth go through the blahs.

This is really important, because a key to minimizing their effects on you is to recognize that you're not alone. What you are going through is universal. There is little reason to get down on yourself.

As the researchers concluded, if you don't do anything, you'll sort of naturally work your way through this. In the same mysterious way that the blahs came upon you, they'll leave. But that can take four or five years—and you don't have to wait that long.

There are two kinds of salespeople in the world: hunters and farmers, aggressive salespeople who go out and actively pursue new business, and the order takers. If you've purchased and read this book, the chances are you fall into the hunter/aggressive salesperson category. That makes everything easier, because it means that you have memories you can call on of better times, of sales you worked your butt off to make. You've had the fire in your belly, and now it's a question of stoking the flames again.

If there is a recurring theme in this book it is that we're all the little engines that could. All we need is the confidence and the memories that remind us: "Yes, I can. Yes, I can. Yes, I can."

AGE BRINGS WISDOM

While some people may think we're over the hill, you and I both know that we possess something naysayers may never have: accumulated wisdom. We know products. We know clients. And we know how to sell. Understanding that will help revive your youthful cockiness.

I know this sounds a little like psychobabble; however, this is more than just wistful wishing to make it so. At least it is once you understand that you're in the catbird's seat.

What you have is rare. How many people do you think have the strength of character and desire to spend twenty, thirty, forty years at a job in which they face the possibility of rejection every single day? And how many of those people can be successful at it day after day, week after week, month after month, and year after year? Certainly not many. And you are in that handful.

What does that mean for you? It means you control your own destiny. The world is yours for the taking. The bottom line is this. You are at or will soon be at a point in your life when money is less important. Your house is likely paid off. Your kids have finished school. I'm not suggesting you retire. The need for cash never ends. If it isn't graduate school for your son it's paying for daughter's wedding. But overall the pressure is off you.

If you don't like what you are doing, you can change it. I won't blow smoke at you. Once you get to be in your forties, fifties, and beyond, the statistics say it becomes progressively more difficult to land a new job. But those statistics cover everyone—including farmers. Look, if you were hiring, would you take on a forty-year-old farmer? Probably not. But you almost certainly will take on a fifty-year-old hunter. The assets you bring to any job are valuable and portable.

But as I've noted here, your wisdom gives you other options as well—from consulting to going into the franchise business you've always dreamed about.

In short, there is no need to go through the midlife blahs. All you need to do is understand how valuable you are in order to recapture the fire in the belly you had . . .

In the beginning.

APPENDIX

Discrimination because of an employee's age is against the law. We all know that. But the truth of the matter is that it still happens. If you interview for the position but don't get the job, is it because you're over 40 (the age at which age discrimination laws kick in) or because the company found a prospect better suited to its needs—who just happens to be younger?

That's the conundrum facing employers, employees, and their attorneys. In fact, even as this is written, the Supreme Court is hearing a case, Meacham v. Knolls Atomic Power Plant Laboratory, which has puzzled many observers.

Knolls Atomic Power Plant Laboratory, part of Lockheed Martin Corporation, fired thirty-one employees, all but one over the age of forty. Supposedly, the guidelines used were the workers' skills and their willingness to retrain.

Most of those over forty banded together and sued, arguing that there was no justification for using an evaluation system that affected older workers so disproportionately. They won their case in a jury trial, but the verdict was overturned in appeal.

The case hinges on the Justices' interpretation of a section of the act that suggests it is okay to adopt policies that place older workers at a disadvantage so long as they are based on "reasonable factors other than age."

In the case before the Supreme Court, the Justices must decide whether it is up to the employer to prove "reasonable factors" exist or the employees who brought the lawsuit to prove that they don't.

A government lawyer arguing for the plaintiffs in the case says "All else being equal, the employer is in better position to explain the reasonableness of its very own business practices."

Defense attorneys, on the otherhand, argue while discrimination based on gender or race is indefensible, age "often does correlate with reasonable employment factors."

This is clearly a slippery slope and whatever the court decides in a real-world situation, sadly employers can always find a reason to hire someone else or fire you. I'd like to end on a more positive note, but that's the truth. That's why it is imperative that you follow the rules in this book and approach your second life with vim, vigor, and the confidence of youth.

For more info, see the Department of Labor website, *www.dol.gov.*

OTHER HELPFUL WEBSITES

From the Equal Employment Opportunity Commission: *www.eeoc.gov* and The AARP has a very helpful, easy-to-understand site: *www.aarp.org.*